I0411552

September 2014

FEDERAL RULEMAKING

Agencies Included Key Elements of Cost-Benefit Analysis, but Explanations of Regulations' Significance Could Be More Transparent

On September 12, 2014, this product was revised to correct the statement in the Highlights referencing the period July 1, 2011 to June 30, 2013.

GAO Highlights

Highlights of GAO-14-714, a report to congressional requesters.

FEDERAL RULEMAKING

Agencies Included Key Elements of Cost-Benefit Analysis, but Explanations of Regulations' Significance Could Be More Transparent

Why GAO Did This Study

Federal agencies issue thousands of regulations each year to achieve national goals. For the few hundred of these rules deemed to be significant, agencies are required to assess expected costs and benefits. For the subset of these rules estimated to have the greatest economic impact, agencies must also include an assessment of alternatives.

GAO was asked to review agencies' compliance with broadly applicable directives and guidance related to significant federal rulemaking. This report addresses (1) how often and to what extent significant, economically significant, and major rules include key elements for assessing or analyzing benefits and costs; and (2) how and to what extent agencies assess the quality of the scientific, technical, and other types of data they use to consider benefits and costs. To answer these objectives, GAO reviewed a generalizable sample of 109 significant and 57 economically significant rules issued by executive agencies and all 37 major rules issued by independent agencies and published in the *Federal Register* from July 1, 2011, to June 30, 2013. GAO also conducted roundtable discussions with the 17 executive and independent agencies with the largest number of rules in GAO's sample.

What GAO Recommends

To improve the transparency of the rulemaking process, GAO recommends the Office of Management and Budget (OMB) work with agencies to clearly communicate why certain rules are designated as significant. OMB staff did not state whether they agreed or disagreed with the recommendation.

View GAO-14-714. For more information, contact Michelle Sager at (202) 512-6806 or sagerm@gao.gov.

What GAO Found

How often and to what extent agencies included selected key elements of cost-benefit analysis varied by rule type. The selected key elements in GAO's review are a statement of purpose; monetized or quantified costs and benefits or a qualitative discussion of them; and a discussion of alternatives. The 203 rules GAO reviewed are categorized into three broad, nonmutually exclusive categories—major, economically significant, and significant rules—based in part on their likely economic effects. Between July 1, 2011, and June 30, 2013, agencies included the selected key elements in the majority of the economically significant and major rules and less often in significant rules. Agencies sometimes included these key elements even when they may not have been required to do so. The results of GAO's review of agencies' regulatory cost-benefit analyses for these rules are as follows:

Statement of purpose: A statement of purpose provides the underlying reason for the rule. Agencies included this element in all rules.

Costs and benefits: Monetizing costs and benefits allows decision makers to evaluate different regulatory options using a common measure. Agencies included a mix of monetized and quantified costs and benefits and qualitative discussions of costs and benefits in most economically significant and major rules, but less often in significant rules. Almost all economically significant rules contained some monetized costs, as did most major rules and some significant rules. Many agency officials said they try to monetize costs and benefits whenever possible, regardless of rule type; however, monetizing benefits can be more difficult than monetizing costs. For example, officials said it is challenging to estimate the value of enhancing national security. Agency officials said that obtaining sufficient or quality data is a primary challenge to cost-benefit analysis.

Alternatives: Analyzing alternatives helps agencies to decide on the best regulatory approach. Agencies identified alternatives in most economically significant and major rules and in some significant rules. Agencies said they sometimes do not identify alternatives because the statute requiring the rule is so specific that considering alternatives is not a practical use of resources.

Agencies included a discussion of how they assessed the data quality more often in economically significant rules than in significant or major rules. Agencies used various methods to assess the data, depending on the type and use of the data. For example, agencies used the peer review process to help ensure science-driven data were the most current and appropriate data available. Only three of the seventeen agencies that participated in GAO's roundtables reported reevaluating cost-benefit analyses once a rule had been issued.

GAO's review also found that for the majority of the 109 significant rules reviewed, the rulemaking process is not as transparent as it could be. This is because 72 percent of these rules included no language to explain why the rule was designated as significant. Some agency officials indicated that the Office of Management and Budget's Office of Information and Regulatory Affairs did not always provide a reason for changing a rule's designation to significant. The rulemaking process could be more transparent if significance designations were explained and communicated.

_____ United States Government Accountability Office

Contents

Figures

Abbreviations

APA	Administrative Procedure Act
CRA	Congressional Review Act
EPA	Environmental Protection Agency
FAR	Federal Acquisition Regulation
GSA	General Services Administration
NLRB	National Labor Relations Board
NRC	Nuclear Regulatory Commission
OIRA	Office of Information and Regulatory Affairs
OMB	Office of Management and Budget
PRA	Paperwork Reduction Act
RFA	Regulatory Flexibility Act
UMRA	Unfunded Mandates Reform Act
WTO GPA	World Trade Organization Government Procurement Agreement

This is a work of the U.S. government and is not subject to copyright protection in the United States. The published product may be reproduced and distributed in its entirety without further permission from GAO. However, because this work may contain copyrighted images or other material, permission from the copyright holder may be necessary if you wish to reproduce this material separately.

441 G St. N.W.
Washington, DC 20548

September 11, 2014

The Honorable Ron Johnson
Ranking Member
Subcommittee on Financial and Contracting Oversight
Committee on Homeland Security and Governmental Affairs
United States Senate

The Honorable Mark R. Warner
Chairman
Task Force on Government Performance
Committee on the Budget
United States Senate

Federal regulations are one of the many tools that agencies use to achieve national goals, such as improving the economy and protecting the health and safety of the public and the environment.[1] While regulations can generate substantial benefits to society, they also have costs. The Office of Management and Budget (OMB) estimated annual benefits from major federal regulations issued in fiscal years 2003 through 2012 to be $193 billion to $800 billion and estimated annual costs of $57 billion to $84 billion.[2] For more than two decades, presidents have issued a number of executive orders directing agencies to analyze the costs and benefits of regulations in order to anticipate and evaluate the likely consequences of rules. OMB's Office of Information and Regulatory Affairs (OIRA) is responsible for ensuring federal regulations issued by agencies, other than independent regulatory agencies, follow executive

---

[1]Regulations are the means by which agencies establish legally binding requirements, and are rooted in agencies' statutory authority. The *Code of Federal Regulations* annual edition is the codification of the general and permanent rules published in the *Federal Register* by the departments and agencies of the federal government. We use the terms regulations and rules interchangeably in this report.

[2]Office of Management and Budget, *2013 Report to Congress on the Benefits and Costs of Federal Regulations and Unfunded Mandates on State, Local, and Tribal Entities,* (Washington, D.C., May, 2014). In these estimates (reported in 2001 dollars), OMB included only the "major" regulations for which agencies estimated and monetized both benefits and costs. OMB noted that the estimates reflect uncertainty of the benefits and costs of each rule at the time it was evaluated. The Congressional Review Act defines "major rules" as those that are likely to result in an annual effect on the economy of $100 million or more, among other criteria. 5 U.S.C. § 804(2).

order requirements for regulatory analysis, including analyzing costs and benefits.[3] The regulatory philosophy and principles of these executive orders recognize that in deciding whether and how to regulate, agencies should assess all costs and benefits of available regulatory alternatives, including the alternative of not regulating.

Executive agencies promulgate thousands of rules each year. In most years, agencies are required to submit only a few hundred of these rules to OIRA for review—only those OIRA has determined are "significant regulatory actions."[4] For these rules, agencies are required to provide OIRA with an assessment of costs and benefits. For a portion of these rules—those with the largest expected economic effects (approximately 17 percent for fiscal years 2003 through 2012)—agencies are required to submit a more detailed analysis of costs and benefits to OIRA, including an analysis of potential alternative regulatory actions.[5] Independent regulatory agencies' rules are not subject to OIRA review, but may have annual economic effects in the hundreds of millions of dollars. A large body of academic and economic research exists on the regulatory analyses (and their cost-benefit analyses) performed on executive agency rules with the largest economic effects. Less is known about rules with smaller economic effects, even though in the aggregate their economic impact can be large.

You asked us to review agencies' compliance with broadly applicable directives and guidance related to significant federal rulemaking. This report addresses (1) how often and to what extent significant rules (including economically significant rules) issued by executive agencies, and major rules issued by independent regulatory agencies, contain key elements for assessing or analyzing benefits and costs; and (2) how and

---

[3]"Independent regulatory agencies" refer to the boards and commissions identified as such in the Paperwork Reduction Act. The Securities and Exchange Commission is one example of an independent regulatory agency. 44 U.S.C. § 3502(5).

[4]Executive agencies are cabinet departments and other agencies that answer directly to the President.

[5]Executive Order No. 12866 requires agencies to submit to OIRA an assessment of the potential costs and benefits of significant regulatory actions. For those rules with the largest expected economic effects (defined as economically significant regulatory actions), agencies must complete a regulatory analysis that includes an assessment, including the underlying analysis, of anticipated costs and benefits. In its review, OIRA generally expects to see more analytical rigor in these economically significant rules.

to what extent agencies assess the quality of the scientific, technical, and other types of data they use to consider costs and benefits.

To answer our first objective, we reviewed 203 final rules that were issued and published in the *Federal Register* between July 1, 2011 and June 30, 2013 to determine whether they contained what we consider (for the purposes of this report) key elements of a cost-benefit analysis: a discussion of the problem the rule intends to address; monetized, quantified, or qualitatively discussed costs; monetized, quantified, or qualitatively discussed benefits; and a discussion of alternatives.[6] These four broad elements stem from several sources including Executive Orders 12866 and 13563, OMB's *Circular A-4,* and general economic principles.[7] *Circular A-4,* consistent with standard economic principles, identifies these selected elements as basic elements to include in the regulatory analysis required by the executive orders.[8] Although other elements could be viewed as key to include in a full and complete regulatory analysis, we focused our review on these selected elements because they are considered to be basic elements important to any

---

[6]For the purposes of this report, we use the term "final rules" to refer to those rules issued by federal agencies and published in the *Federal Register* as final regulatory actions. For the list of rules we reviewed as part of our sample, see app. II.

[7]Exec. Order No. 12866, *Regulatory Planning and Review*, 58 Fed. Reg. 51,735 (Oct. 4, 1993). President Obama reaffirmed the regulatory principles, structures, and definitions of Executive Order 12866 in Exec. Order No. 13563, *Improving Regulation and Regulatory Review*, 76 Fed. Reg. 3821 (Jan. 21, 2011). In this report, when we refer to Exec. Order No. 12866, we also include the subsequent and related updates in Exec. Order No. 13563. OMB *Circular A-4* provides guidance to federal agencies on the development of regulatory analysis and is designed to assist agencies in standardizing the way costs and benefits of federal regulatory actions are measured and reported.

[8]Including these key elements may also help agencies address similar elements in various statutory rulemaking requirements, such as the Administrative Procedure Act (APA) and the Unfunded Mandates Reform Act (UMRA). For example, the APA, which spells out the basic process by which agencies develop and issue regulations, provides that "the agency shall incorporate in the rules adopted a concise general statement of their basis and purpose." 5 U.S.C. § 553(c). UMRA generally requires federal agencies to prepare a written statement containing a "qualitative and quantitative assessment of the anticipated costs and benefits" for any rule that includes a federal mandate that may result in the expenditure of $100 million or more (adjusted for inflation) in any 1 year by state, local, and tribal governments in the aggregate, or by the private sector. In 2014, the dollar threshold is $152 million. For such rules, agencies are to identify and consider a reasonable number of regulatory alternatives and from those, to select the least costly, most cost-effective, or least burdensome alternative that achieves the objectives of the rule (or explain why that alternative was not selected). 2 U.S.C. §§ 1532, 1535.

regulatory cost-benefit assessment and analysis. We recognize that agencies were not required to include all of the key elements for all of the rule types we reviewed and that it may not always be feasible to include all key elements in a rule. Further, our analysis was not designed to evaluate the quality of the cost-benefit analysis in the rules. The presence of all key elements does not provide information regarding the quality of the analysis, nor does the absence of a key element necessarily imply a deficiency in a cost-benefit analysis.

Although rules may fall into multiple categories—such as being both economically significant and major—we divided our analysis into three distinct categories: economically significant, significant, and major. For the purposes of this report, we include economically significant rules in our sample separately from significant rules. While executive agency rules can be major, in our sample for this report, they were also all economically significant. In this report, we use the term major rules to mean only those major rules issued by independent regulatory agencies. For significant and economically significant rules, we reviewed a stratified random sample drawn from the full population of final rules of both types issued between July 1, 2011 and June 30, 2013. We reviewed 109 significant rules and 57 economically significant rules. Estimates of these populations are based on these sample data and are subject to sampling error.[9] We also reviewed the population of all 37 major rules issued by independent regulatory agencies within the same time frame. Values reported for those rules are not subject to sampling error and are not estimates but population values.

To supplement the rule review and to answer our second objective, we conducted roundtable discussions with 17 of the 32 independent

---

[9]In this report, margins of error for the point estimates for the full population are within ±7 percentage points at the 95 percent confidence level, unless otherwise noted.

GAO-14-714 Federal Rulemaking

regulatory and executive agencies that issued the rules we reviewed.[10] At these roundtables, we asked the agency officials involved in the development of agency regulations to discuss their interactions with OIRA, the challenges they face in including the select key elements of cost-benefit analyses, the steps they take to assess the quality of their data, and how often (if at all) they compare estimated costs and benefits in rules to outcome data after rules are implemented. At the executive agency roundtables, we asked agency officials to compare their approaches to cost-benefit analyses in significant and economically significant rules. Further information about our rule review sample and roundtables can be found in appendix I.

We conducted this performance audit from June 2013 to September 2014 in accordance with generally accepted government auditing standards. Those standards require that we plan and perform the audit to obtain sufficient, appropriate evidence to provide a reasonable basis for our findings and conclusions based on our audit objectives. We believe that the evidence obtained provides a reasonable basis for our findings and conclusions based on our audit objectives.

Background

The Paperwork Reduction Act of 1980 (PRA) established OIRA as an office within OMB.[11] OIRA is responsible for the coordinated review of executive agency rulemakings to ensure that regulations are consistent with applicable laws, the President's priorities, and the principles set forth

---

[10]Thirty-two agencies had final rules that were issued in our sample's time period. We chose agencies to participate in our roundtables based on how frequently the agencies' rules appeared in our sample. The following agencies participated in our roundtable discussions: Commodity Futures Trading Commission, Consumer Financial Protection Bureau, Consumer Product Safety Commission, Department of Commerce, Department of Defense, Department of Education, Department of Health and Human Services, Department of the Interior, Department of Labor, Department of Transportation, Environmental Protection Agency, Federal Communications Commission, Federal Reserve System, General Services Administration, National Labor Relations Board, Nuclear Regulatory Commission, and Securities and Exchange Commission. The Federal Acquisition Regulation (FAR) is issued jointly by the General Services Administration (GSA), Department of Defense, and the National Aeronautics and Space Administration. GSA's participation was specifically to discuss the FAR and not to discuss rules issued solely by GSA; Department of Defense participants discussed both the FAR and other defense regulations.

[11]44 U.S.C. § 3503(a). PRA was originally enacted into law in 1980, Pub. L. No. 96-511, 94 Stat. 2812 (1980).

in executive orders. Agencies provide OIRA with basic summary information when drafting rules to determine if additional OIRA review is required. If so, agencies provide any required analyses (including information on estimated costs and benefits) to OIRA before issuing a final rule. OIRA desk officers review the rule and related documents and may request changes or additional analyses. Further, OIRA is responsible for ensuring that decisions made by one agency do not conflict with the policies or actions taken or planned by another agency.

OMB also provides guidance to agencies on the development of regulatory analysis, of which cost-benefit analysis is a primary tool. According to Executive Order 12866, OIRA is to be the repository of expertise concerning regulatory issues. OIRA is also responsible under PRA for reviewing all information collections by the federal government.[12] Independent regulatory agencies are not subject to OIRA regulatory review, although OIRA does interact with these agencies on other regulatory matters, such as approving information collections and making major rule determinations.

Several laws, executive orders, and OMB guidance provide direction for agencies in the rulemaking process and impose requirements on agencies, depending on the type of rule being promulgated.[13] These laws and executive orders also define four broad categories of rules. These categories—which are not necessarily mutually exclusive—are major, significant, economically significant, and non-major/non-significant.

[12]Under PRA, generally all agencies, including independent regulatory agencies, are required to submit proposed information collections to OIRA. 44 U.S.C. § 3504. Information collections generally cover information obtained from more than ten sources. 44 U.S.C. § 3502(3)(A). In their submissions, agencies must establish the need and intended use of the information, estimate the burden that the collection will impose on respondents, and show that the collection is the least burdensome way to gather the information. 44 U.S.C. § 3506(c), 5 C.F.R. § 1320.11.

[13]For a summary of common regulatory requirements, see app. I of GAO, *Federal Rulemaking: Improvements Needed to Monitoring and Evaluation of Rules Development as Well as to the Transparency of OMB Regulatory Reviews*, GAO-09-205 (Washington, D.C.: Apr. 20, 2009). For an overview of key requirements for regulatory retrospective analysis, see app. I of GAO, *Reexamining Regulations: Agencies Often Made Regulatory Changes, but Could Strengthen Linkages to Performance Goals*, GAO-14-268 (Washington, D.C.: Apr. 11, 2014).

Major rules are defined by the Congressional Review Act (CRA).[14] CRA applies to both executive and independent regulatory agencies. Major rules are those that will likely result in

- an annual effect on the economy of $100 million or more, or
- major increases in costs or prices for consumers, individual industries, federal, state, or local government agencies, or geographic regions, or
- significant adverse effects on competition, employment, investment, productivity, or innovation, or on the ability of United States-based enterprises to compete with foreign-based enterprises in domestic and export markets.

Under CRA, OIRA is responsible for making major rule designations for both executive and independent regulatory agencies.[15] Rules that are not designated as major are referred to as non-major.

Significant and economically significant rules are defined in Executive Order 12866 for executive agencies. In addition to being major or non-major, executive agency rules are also identified as significant, economically significant, or non-significant regulatory actions under Executive Order 12866. According to OMB, the majority of rules issued every year by executive agencies are not significant regulatory actions. These regulatory actions may include rules that affect a small number of individuals or entities or only affect agency operations.[16]

A rule is significant under Executive Order 12866 if it meets one of the following four criteria:

- The rule is likely to have an annual effect on the economy of $100 million or more or adversely affect in a material way the economy, a sector of the economy, productivity, competition, jobs, the environment, public health or safety, or state, local, or tribal governments or communities.
- The rule is likely to create a serious inconsistency or otherwise interfere with an action taken or planned by another agency.

---

[14]5 U.S.C. § 804(2).

[15]*Id.*

[16]According to OMB, during fiscal years 2003 through 2012, federal agencies published, on average, 3,779 final regulations each year. Executive agencies issued on average 320 significant rules a year, including approximately 54 major rules annually.

- The rule is likely to materially alter the budgetary impact of entitlements, grants, user fees, or loan programs or the rights and obligations of recipients thereof.
- The rule is likely to raise novel legal or policy issues arising out of legal mandates, the President's priorities, or the principles set forth in Executive Order 12866.

Economically significant rules, a subset of significant rules, are those that meet the first criteria above for significant rules. The definition of economically significant is largely similar to the definition of major rules.[17] Only executive agency rules can be classified as economically significant, but both executive agencies and independent regulatory agencies can issue major rules. Generally, economically significant rules issued by executive agencies are also classified as major rules. Figure 1, an interactive graphic, shows the relationship between significant and economically significant rules for executive agencies.

---

[17]Major and economically significant rules are subject to the same $100 million economic effect threshold, but vary in that the definition of major is broader than that of economically significant. Rules that may be designated as major under CRA but not economically significant under Executive Order 12866 include those that would have a significant adverse effect on the ability of United States-based enterprises to compete with foreign-based enterprises in domestic and export markets. All but one of the economically significant rules we reviewed for this report were also designated as major under CRA.

Figure 1: Rule Type Definitions for Executive Agency Rules

Directions:

Roll over Significant, Economically Significant, and Major to see more information regarding the rules and executive orders guidance category groupings used by agencies.

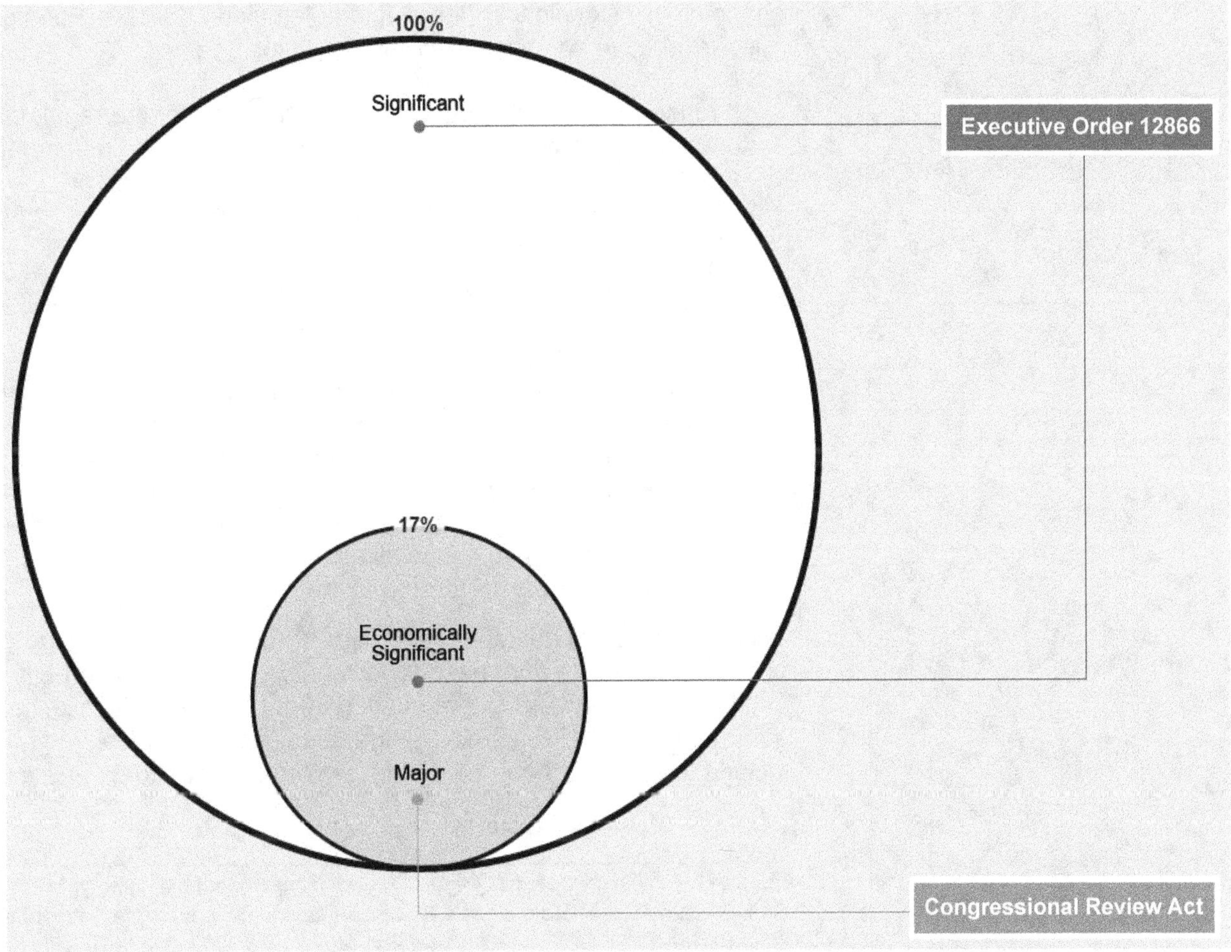

100%

Significant ———————————————— **Executive Order 12866**

17%

Economically
Significant ——————

Major ——

Congressional Review Act

Source: GAO analysis of Executive Order 12866 and the Congressional Review Act. | GAO-14-714

Note: This figure reflects rules issued only by executive agencies and does not include major rules issued by independent regulatory agencies. During fiscal years 2003 through 2012, approximately 17 percent of the significant regulations issued by executive agencies were also considered economically significant or major.

Print instructions | To print text version of this graphic, go to appendix IV.

Requirements for Regulatory Analysis and Oversight

Executive Order 12866 promotes a regulatory philosophy and set of principles that, to the extent permitted by law and where applicable, encourages agencies to assess costs, benefits, and available regulatory alternatives in all rules, including the alternative of not regulating. Executive Order 13563 reaffirms this philosophy and these principles.[18] These executive orders include more specific requirements for some agencies and some rules. Executive agencies are required to include certain information about the costs and benefits of significant and economically significant rules in final rulemaking dockets. For significant rules, executive agencies are required to include

- a reasonably detailed description of the need for the regulatory action and an explanation of how the regulatory action will meet that need, and
- an assessment of the potential costs and benefits of the regulatory action.[19]

For economically significant rules, executive agencies are further required to include

- an assessment, including the underlying analysis, of the costs and benefits anticipated from the regulatory action, with, to the extent feasible, a quantification of those costs and benefits; and
- an assessment, including the underlying analysis, of costs and benefits of potentially effective and reasonably feasible alternatives to the planned regulation, as well as an explanation of why the planned regulatory action is preferable to the identified alternatives.[20]

According to OMB guidance, agencies should consider a range of potentially effective and reasonably feasible regulatory alternatives when analyzing alternatives. The relevant alternatives might involve different approaches, with distinct advantages and disadvantages, and may include the option of not regulating, among other options. Agencies can

---

[18]President Clinton issued Exec. Order No. 12866 in 1993. In January 2011, President Obama issued Exec. Order No. 13563 which reaffirmed the principles, structures, and definitions governing regulatory review that were established in Exec. Order No. 12866, as well as established additional regulatory requirements, including requirements specific to regulatory retrospective analyses. For more information on regulatory retrospective analyses, see GAO-14-268.

[19]Exec. Order No. 12866, § 6(a)(3)(B).

[20]Exec. Order No. 12866, § 6(a)(3)(C).

also analyze alternatives with varying enforcement methods, stringency requirements, compliance dates, or requirements based on firm size or geographic location.

Independent regulatory agencies are not subject to Executive Order 12866 requirements. However, these independent regulatory agencies, as well as executive agencies, may be subject to other statutory provisions that require the agencies to include certain types of analyses in rules, including costs and benefits. For example, all agencies, including independent regulatory agencies, must meet the requirements of PRA,[21] the Regulatory Flexibility Act (RFA) (impact on small entities),[22] and executive agencies must meet the requirements of the Unfunded Mandates Reform Act (UMRA) in certain circumstances.[23] In addition, executive and independent regulatory agencies may have agency-specific statutory requirements for assessing or analyzing costs, benefits, or alternatives.[24] Table 1 summarizes definitions of rule types and select requirements for regulatory analysis.

[21]See note 12 *infra*.

[22]5 U.S.C. §§ 601-612.

[23]Pub. L. No. 104-4, 109 Stat. 48 (1995) (Codified in scattered sections of title 2 of the United States Code). *See* note 8 *infra*.

[24]For example, the Commodity Futures Trading Commission, under section 15(a) of the Commodity Exchange Act, is required to consider the benefits and costs of its action before promulgating a regulation or issuing certain orders. Section 15(a) specifies that the benefits and costs shall be evaluated in light of (1) protection of market participants and the public; (2) efficiency, competitiveness, and financial integrity of futures markets; (3) price discovery; (4) sound risk-management practices; and (5) other public interest considerations. (Codified as amended at 7 U.S.C. § 19(a)).

Table 1: Summary of Selected Definitions and Requirements of Executive Order 12866 and the Congressional Review Act

	Significant rules[a]	Economically significant rules	Major rules
Defined by	Executive Order 12866	Executive Order 12866	Congressional Review Act
Definition	Likely to • interfere with another agency's actions, • materially alter the budgetary impact of entitlements, grants, user fees, or loan programs or the rights and obligations of recipients thereof, or • raise novel legal or policy issues.	Likely to • have an annual effect on the economy of $100 million or more, or • adversely affect the economy, productivity, competition, jobs, the environment, public health or safety, or state, local, or tribal governments or communities.	Likely to • have an annual effect on the economy of $100 million or more, • cause major increases in costs or prices, or • have significant adverse effects on competition, employment, investment, productivity, or innovation.
Definition applies to	Executive agencies	Executive agencies	Executive and independent regulatory agencies
Cost-benefit analysis requirements	Executive Order 12866 directs agencies issuing rules that meet the criteria of significant regulatory actions to • describe the need for the action and explain how the action will meet that need, and • assess potential costs and benefits of the regulatory action. Significant rules may be subject to additional statutory requirements for assessing costs, benefits, or alternatives that may not apply to every rule.	In addition to the requirements for significant rules, Executive Order 12866 directs agencies issuing rules that meet the criteria of economically significant regulatory actions to also • quantify costs and benefits when feasible, and • assess costs and benefits of feasible alternatives and explain why the planned action is preferable to the alternative. Economically significant rules may be subject to additional statutory requirements for assessing costs, benefits, or alternatives that may not apply to every rule.	In addition to the requirements for executive agencies in Executive Order 12866, major rules issued by executive and independent regulatory agencies may be subject to statutory requirements for assessing costs, benefits, or alternatives. The Congressional Review Act requires executive and independent regulatory agencies to submit any cost-benefit analyses to the Congress and GAO.

Source: GAO analysis of Executive Order 12866 and the Congressional Review Act. | GAO-14-714

Note:

[a]Economically significant rules are a subset of significant rules. For the purposes of this table, significant rules exclude the subset of economically significant rules, which is defined and discussed separately.

Circular A-4 was issued by OMB in 2003 to provide guidance and best practices to federal agencies on conducting regulatory analyses.[25] Cost-benefit analysis, the primary tool of regulatory analysis, can provide government agencies, Congress, and the public with important

---

[25]*Circular A-4* replaced OMB's "best practices" document of 1996, which was issued as guidance in 2000 and reaffirmed in 2001.

information about the potential effects of new regulations.[26] *Circular A-4* offers a framework for how agencies can analyze the costs and benefits of a proposed regulation, but generally does not prescribe the specific assumptions or values to use in analyzing the potential effects of rules. This flexibility is intended to allow agencies to apply the framework to their particular regulations and regulated entities. According to *Circular A-4*, a good regulatory analysis should include three basic elements: a statement of the need for the proposed action; an examination of alternative approaches; and an evaluation of the benefits and costs (quantitative and qualitative) of the proposed action and the main alternatives identified by the analysis. OIRA uses *Circular A-4* as the primary guidance in reviewing regulatory analyses. Figure 2, an interactive graphic, shows how OIRA's review and requirements for regulatory analyses differ based on the type of agency and rule.

---

[26]Exec. Order No. 12866 requires agencies to assess costs and benefits of significant rules and, for economically significant rules, to analyze the costs and benefits of the rule and of reasonably feasible alternatives. For the purposes of this report, we use the term "cost-benefit" analysis to include both the assessment of costs and benefits for significant rules and the more rigorous requirements for economically significant rules.

Figure 2: Office of Information and Regulatory Affairs (OIRA) Review Process for Significant, Economically Significant, and Major Rules under Executive Order 12866 and the Congressional Review Act

Directions:

Click On each decision point (1) **Executive Agency**, (2) **Significant**, (3) **Economically Significant**, and (4) **Independent Agency** to see the separate rule review flow process for each action **Move-Off** to see the full process flow.

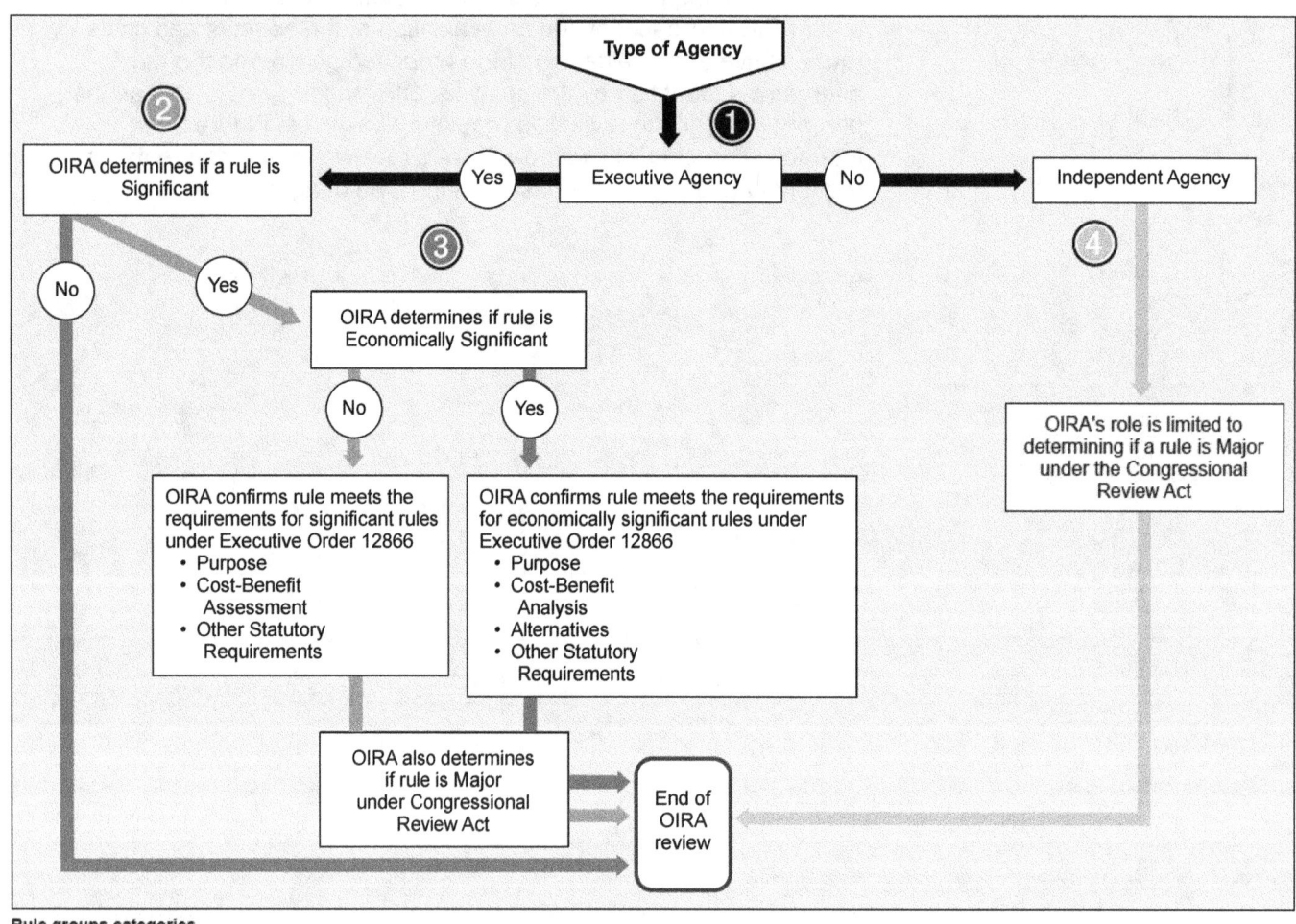

Rule groups categories

◯ Major   ◯ Significant   ● Economically Significant

Source: GAO analysis of Executive Order 12866 and Congressional Review Act. | GAO-14-714

Note: Criteria and requirements for significant and economically significant rules are derived from Exec. Order Nos. 12866 and 13563. Criteria for major rules are derived from the Congressional Review Act.

As shown in figure 2, one step in regulatory analysis is for an agency to determine if a rule is a major rule under the CRA, a significant regulatory action under Executive Order 12866, or both. Under CRA, OIRA is responsible for determining if rules are major for all agencies, including independent regulatory agencies. Executive agencies must also determine if their rules are significant regulatory actions, including determining whether the rules are economically significant and OIRA must concur. OIRA determines if independent regulatory agencies' rules are major before the rules are issued.[27]

Agencies Included Key Elements of Cost-Benefit Analysis in the Majority of Economically Significant and Major Rules and in about Half of Significant Rules, but Information on Rule Designation Lacked Transparency

---

[27] In our December 2013 report, we found that this process of designating a rule as major is not clear for some independent regulatory agencies and we recommended that OIRA issue additional guidance to help standardize the process for identifying major rules at these agencies. See GAO, *Dodd-Frank Regulations: Agencies Conducted Regulatory Analyses and Coordinated but Could Benefit from Additional Guidance on Major Rules,* GAO-14-67 (Washington, D.C.: Dec. 11, 2013).

Agencies and OIRA Are Not Always Transparent about How Rules Are Designated

OIRA staff told us that executive agencies typically make a preliminary assessment of a rule's designation as significant or not when planning their regulatory actions.[28] The 109 significant (excluding economically significant) rules we reviewed ranged from those implementing minor, low-cost technical changes to those with economic effects just under the (economically significant) $100 million threshold; these rules generally contained a section describing the actions taken by the agency to fulfill regulatory requirements and a statement of whether the rule was a significant regulatory action or not. However, 72 percent of these significant rules lacked specific language to explain why they were designated as significant. Agencies did not include this information when drafting the rules, and OIRA did not require it to be included when they reviewed the rules.[29] A few agencies told us that they did not always have the reason for the significance determination from OIRA.

OIRA staff told us that OIRA usually agrees with agency determinations about a rule's significance and that OIRA staff generally discuss the basis for their significance determinations with agency officials. However, agency officials said that OIRA has at times changed the agencies' designation of some rules from non-significant to significant and that OIRA does not always provide a reason when it does so. Agency officials said that when OIRA does not tell them the reason why the rules are designated as significant, some officials assume the reason for a changed designation could be due to OIRA's consideration of the rule as "likely to raise novel legal or policy issues," one of the four categories of significant rules.[30] (One agency's officials said it was to ensure the rule is circulated to other agencies for comment.)

---

[28]Significant rules that are not also economically significant include rules that are likely to create a serious inconsistency or otherwise interfere with an action taken or planned by another agency; materially alter the budgetary impact of entitlements, grants, user fees, or loan programs or the rights and obligations of recipients thereof; or raise novel legal or policy issues arising out of legal mandates, the President's priorities, or the principles set forth in Exec. Order No. 12866. For the purposes of our analysis, when we discuss significant rules, we include those rules that are significant, but not economically significant.

[29]While Exec. Order No. 12866 defines significant rules, there is no requirement that agencies publish in their rules which criteria designates the rule as significant.

[30]The rule is likely to raise novel legal or policy issues arising out of legal mandates, the President's priorities, or the principles set forth in Executive Order 12866. Exec. Order No. 12866, § 3(f)(4).

Officials from some executive agencies told us that recently OIRA has more frequently changed the designation of rules. Some agency officials said that changes in rule designation can vary by agency or by OIRA desk officer (the staff at OIRA who review agency rule designations). For example, officials from one agency told us that OIRA changes the designation of its agency's rules about 50 percent of the time, while officials from another agency said OIRA rarely disagreed with their agency's initial designation. OIRA staff told us that there can be variation across agencies because agencies vary in the types of regulations they issue and the desk officers assigned to each agency have discretion to determine how OMB requirements apply to a rule.

One of Executive Order 12866's objectives is to make the regulatory process more accessible and open to the public; however, a lack of consistent information explaining why a rule is designated as significant prevents policymakers and the public from knowing how OIRA is applying criteria for designating significant regulatory actions. If agencies do not know the reason why their original assessment of the rule's designation is changed, then they lack full information to include in their final rules and to better plan future regulatory actions. Federal standards for internal controls state that effective information and communication is vital for an entity to run and control its operations. Agency management should ensure there are adequate means of communications with external stakeholders that can have a significant impact on the agency achieving its goals.[31] OMB has also stressed the need for transparency in agency decisions.[32] When OIRA changes the designation of a rule from non-significant to significant, it can result in additional regulatory analysis requirements for agencies, which may prolong the rulemaking process; however, it may also provide the agency, Congress, and the public with additional information about potential costs and benefits of the rule, enhancing decision making and oversight.

[31]GAO, *Standards for Internal Control in the Federal Government*, GAO/AIMD-00-21.3.1 (Washington, D.C.: November 1999).

[32]Office of Management and Budget, *Open Government Directive*, M-10-06, December 8, 2009.

Agencies' Inclusion of Select Key Elements Varied by Rule Type

Our review of 203 rules found that agencies included at least three of the four select key elements in the majority of economically significant rules issued by executive agencies and major rules issued by independent regulatory agencies between July 1, 2011 and June 30, 2013.[33] Executive agencies included the key elements less frequently in significant rules. For the purpose of this report, we define the key elements of cost-benefit analysis in four broad categories as a statement of purpose; monetized, quantified, or qualitatively discussed costs; monetized, quantified, or qualitatively discussed benefits; and a discussion of alternatives. Table 2 shows the extent to which agencies included the select key elements.[34] We discuss the inclusion of each key element later in this report.

Table 2: Percentage of Federal Rules that Included Selected Key Elements of Cost-Benefit Analysis by Rule Type - July 1, 2011 to June 30, 2013

Total number of key elements included: purpose, costs, benefits, alternatives	Percentage of significant rules from executive agencies that included key elements	Percentage of economically significant rules from executive agencies that included key elements	Percentage of major rules from independent regulatory agencies that included key elements
4 elements	19[a]	81[b]	57[c]
3 elements	31	19	41
2 elements	25	0	0
1 element	25	0	3

Source: GAO analysis of federal regulations. | GAO-14-714.

Notes

[a]For significant rules, we reviewed a sample of 109 rules from the population of 284 rules, and generalized to that population. Margins of error for the point estimates for the full population are within ±7 percentage points at the 95 percent confidence level. For example, an estimated 19 percent of significant rules contained all 4 key elements we identified, and we are 95 percent confident that the actual value is within ±7 percentage points of this estimate.

[b]For economically significant rules, we reviewed a sample of 57 rules from the population of 78, and generalized to that population. Margins of error for the percentage estimates for the full population are within ±6 percentage points at the 95 percent confidence level.

[33]Although executive agencies' rules can also be designated as major, for the purposes of our analysis and this report, when we refer to major rules we mean only those major rules issued by independent regulatory agencies.

[34]Percentage estimates for the significant and economically significant rules have 95 percent confidence intervals that are within ±7 percentage points of the estimate itself, unless otherwise noted. For major rules from independent agencies, we reviewed the full population of rules issued within our time period; therefore, these values are not estimates. For more information on sampling error for estimates provided in this report, see appendix III.

°For major rules issued by independent regulatory agencies, we reviewed the full population of 37 rules. Percentages in this table for major rules are actual values and not estimates. Percentages may not add to 100 due to rounding.

Executive orders and OIRA guidance acknowledge there that are instances when including a key element in a rule is not feasible or may be prohibited by law. According to OIRA staff, in its review of executive agencies' significant and economically significant regulatory actions, OIRA starts with the expectation that all rules will include the required elements of cost-benefit analysis. According to OIRA staff, this is true even for rules that stem from prescriptive statutes. However, during its review OIRA allows agencies to apply a "rule of reason" to determine whether it is acceptable to not contain elements that would typically be expected in cost-benefit analysis. These decisions are made on a case-by-case basis. As described to us by OIRA staff, the "rule of reason" acknowledges that agencies face constraints, including resource limitations, data limitations, and sometimes, prohibitive statutory language. According to OIRA staff, OIRA and the agencies must balance the benefit of including the key elements with case-specific limitations and agency resources. OIRA and the agencies also consider the expected economic effect of a rule when making decisions about the extent of analysis required. OIRA staff said that OIRA desk officers expect to see a more rigorous analysis in rules with greater expected economic effects. For example, OIRA generally expects a significant rule with an expected annual economic effect of $90 million to have a more thorough assessment of costs and benefits than a rule with an expected annual economic effect of $1 million.

Executive and independent regulatory agency officials cited several reasons why some rules may not contain one or more of the selected key elements. If the rule is required by a statute that is so prescriptive as to leave the agency little or no discretion in the rulemaking process, agencies may decide not to analyze alternatives. For example, rules issued to amend the Federal Acquisition Regulation generally implement statute, executive order, or other agencies' regulations with little room for discretion.[35] Some independent regulatory agency officials also told us

---

[35]The Department of Defense, General Services Administration, and the National Aeronautics and Space Administration jointly issue the Federal Acquisition Regulation (FAR). The FAR System governs the acquisition process and provides uniform policies and practices for agencies' use in purchasing products and services to meet agency missions. It also regulates the activities of contractors and government personnel participating in the acquisition process.

there are sometimes statutory limits on the types of costs, benefits, or alternatives the agency can consider in the rulemaking process. We did not discuss individual rules with the agencies or with OIRA to identify the specific reasons why some rules in our sample did not include all four of the key elements.

Agency officials that we spoke with reported that regardless of rule type, they generally attempt to include the key elements of cost-benefit analysis in final rules. Executive agency officials told us that they approach cost-benefit analyses in the same manner, regardless of whether the rules are economically significant and required by Executive Order 12866 to include a full cost-benefit analysis, or whether they are significant, with the narrower requirement in the Executive Order to provide OIRA with an assessment of costs and benefits of the proposed regulatory action (and with no requirement to provide an analysis of other alternatives.) One executive agency emphasized that they apply the same methodological approach for both the economic and science portions of their analyses, regardless of rule type. For both types of rules, executive agency officials said they include these key elements whenever possible. Independent regulatory agency officials also said that they include the selected key elements of cost-benefit analysis to the extent possible, even though they are not subject to Executive Order 12866. However, independent regulatory agencies may be subject to other statutory requirements that include some requirements to conduct assessment or analysis of potential costs and benefits during rulemaking.[36]

Executive and independent regulatory agency officials reported that they recognize the importance of regulatory and cost-benefit analysis and dedicate considerable time and resources to completing such analyses. For example, some agency officials told us they have economists with expertise in cost-benefit analysis on staff or they hire contractors to supplement in-house staff or to provide analyses when agencies lack the expertise internally. Some agencies also told us they have centralized review processes to ensure consistency in their approaches to cost-benefit analyses. Some agency officials also told us they look to OIRA for additional support, as necessary, when conducting cost-benefit analyses.

---

[36]See note 24 *infra.*

Agency officials we spoke with, including from some independent regulatory agencies, told us that they used OMB's *Circular A-4* guidance, either alone or in conjunction with other agency-specific internal guidance, when conducting cost-benefit analysis. Some executive and independent regulatory agency officials told us that they found *Circular A-4* guidance helpful because its flexibility helps them include the key elements of cost-benefit analysis in many different types of rules. Some officials also told us that they regularly consult with OIRA (through formal and informal exchanges) for technical assistance when conducting cost-benefit analyses. Independent regulatory agencies are not subject to OIRA's regulatory review, but officials from a few independent regulatory agencies stated that, at times, they have reached out to OIRA for technical assistance in completing cost-benefit analyses. Other agency officials also told us that they use *Circular A-4,* but that they sometimes find the guidance too broad to apply to some of their more technical rules.

All Agencies Included a Statement of Purpose As the Starting Point for Their Cost-Benefit Analyses

Key Element: Statement of Purpose

A statement of purpose provides the starting point for discussing what the agency intends to accomplish and the underlying reason for the rule, namely, how it is required by law or is made necessary by some compelling public need. Further, a statement of purpose provides a basis for evaluating whether the regulation successfully accomplished its goal. In final rules, it is required by the Administrative Procedures Act.

Source: GAO analysis of Executive Order 12866, *Circular A-4*, Administrative Procedures Act, and general economic principles.

All agencies included a statement of purpose in the 203 rules we reviewed.[37] We define a statement of purpose as a clear discussion of the need or issue the regulatory action intended to address. Agencies may issue rules because they are directed to do so, such as by statute or by judicial or presidential directive. For example, in response to a presidential directive, the Department of State issued a rule amending the International Traffic in Arms Regulations and listing Afghanistan as a major non-NATO ally.[38] Agencies may also issue rules to address a market failure or to address some other compelling public need, such as improving the functioning of the government or promoting privacy and personal freedom. For example, the Department of Homeland Security issued a rule in January 2013 amending certain immigration regulations in order to reduce the time U.S. citizens are separated from their immediate relatives who are applying for lawful permanent residence status, and to create greater efficiencies for both the government and certain immigration applicants.[39]

Purpose statements provide agencies with a basis for evaluating whether the regulation successfully accomplished its goal, and aids in identifying expected benefits.[40] Officials from one agency told us that the precise purpose of a mandatory rule is not always clear from the statutory text and its legislative history, which can affect the assessment of the benefits of the rule.

---

[37] Based on our sample, we estimated that 100 percent of the rules included a statement of purpose. For this estimate, our 95 percent confidence interval is from 98 percent to 100 percent.

[38] 77 Fed. Reg. 76,864 (Dec. 31. 2012).

[39] 78 Fed. Reg. 536 (Jan. 3, 2013).

[40] In retrospective analyses, agencies assess existing regulations for a variety of purposes, including determining whether the expected outcomes of a regulation have been achieved. See GAO-14-268.

Agencies Included a Mix of Monetized, Quantified, and Qualitatively Discussed Costs and Benefits in Certain Rules but Monetizing All Costs and Benefits Was Challenging

Key Elements: Costs and Benefits

An evaluation of costs and benefits provides a systematic framework for identifying and assessing the economic tradeoffs associated with alternative regulatory choices.

Source: GAO analysis of Executive Order 12866, *Circular A-4*, and general economic principles.

Agencies can assess and analyze costs and benefits both quantitatively—such as expressing a benefit in terms of number of accidents prevented—and qualitatively, such as by describing the benefit of providing consumers with additional information. According to OMB, monetizing costs and benefits, where feasible, allows decision makers to compare the benefits and costs of different regulatory options, using a common measure of value (e.g., dollars). For example, when all costs and benefits are monetized for a proposed rule and an alternative, decision makers can compare the different options and choose the one that is expected to maximize net benefits. According to *Circular A-4*, in the absence of monetization, agencies should still attempt to quantify all costs and benefits whenever possible. If costs or benefits cannot be quantified, agencies should discuss them qualitatively. *Circular A-4* also directs agencies to include a discussion of the strengths and limitations of any quantitative or qualitative information used in lieu of monetization. Executive Order 12866 directs agencies to assess costs and benefits for significant rules and to complete a more rigorous analysis of costs and benefits for economically significant rules. Some independent regulatory agencies may have specific statutory requirements for assessing costs and benefits, which may vary by rule or agency. We found that rules often contained a mix of monetized, quantified, and qualitatively discussed costs and benefits.[41] For example, an agency may identify that there will be costs associated with developing new business practices, quantify the number of illnesses prevented, and monetize the fixed costs for a business to install new equipment.

According to our analysis, executive agencies monetized costs in about 97 percent of economically significant rules and in about 39 percent of significant rules. Independent regulatory agencies monetized costs in about 78 percent of major rules. In addition to monetized costs, our analysis showed that executive agencies monetized benefits in about 76 percent of economically significant rules and in about 16 percent of significant rules. Independent regulatory agencies included monetized benefits in about 5 percent of their major rules. Although we did not assess whether the agencies identified all the appropriate costs and benefits that would be generated by their rules or whether all identified costs and benefits were amenable to monetization, our sample of rules

---

[41]Qualitatively discussed costs and benefits are those costs and benefits that are identified and discussed but are not quantified or monetized.

showed that executive agencies monetized all identified costs in about 42 percent of economically significant rules and in about 23 percent of significant rules. Independent regulatory agencies did so in about 3 percent of their major rules. Agencies monetized all identified benefits in fewer instances. We found executive agencies monetized all identified benefits in about 20 percent of economically significant rules and in about 4 percent of significant rules. Independent regulatory agencies had no rules where all identified benefits were monetized.

Agency officials said that they try to monetize costs and benefits whenever feasible, regardless of rule type, and many agency officials told us monetizing benefits is more difficult than monetizing costs. Several agencies described the difficulty of monetizing benefits such as enhancements to national security, the value of new information to consumers, or the protection of an endangered species. Some agency officials (whose regulations aim to prevent workplace or consumer product accidents) told us that while they may have the ability to monetize the value of preventing one accident, they face difficulties in estimating how many accidents a particular regulation will prevent, given general uncertainties about regulatory effectiveness as well as potential changes in consumer behavior. Officials from one agency further stated that it issues regulations that create redundant systems to prevent injuries; identifying the costs and benefits of each step in isolation is difficult.

Our analysis showed that most rules did not include a calculation of net benefits. A net benefits calculation compares all costs to all benefits to show if the total benefits justify the total costs. For example, the Department of Energy monetized all identified costs and benefits in a rule on energy conservation standards for fluorescent lamp ballasts, and expressed these costs and benefits in a table highlighting the calculated net benefits.[42] In some instances when rules did not monetize all costs or benefits, agencies presented net benefit information along with qualitative cost or benefit information. For example, the Department of Commerce's Patent and Trademark Office compared the qualitative costs and benefits of its new patent fee schedule along with the monetized costs and benefits; the net benefits were determined to be positive and significant, even though the analysis did not monetize all costs and benefits.[43]

---

[42] 76 Fed. Reg. 70,548 (Nov. 14, 2011).

[43] 78 Fed. Reg. 4212 (Jan. 18, 2013).

According to our analysis, executive agencies provided a net benefits calculation in an estimated 37 percent of economically significant rules and an estimated 6 percent of significant rules. Independent regulatory agencies did not include a net benefits calculation in any of their major rules.

In the rules without net benefits calculations, some agencies included statements indicating a determination that the rule's estimated benefits justified the estimated costs; however, they did not always provide additional information in the rule to support the statement. When rules did not include net benefits calculations, agencies sometimes included threshold or break-even analyses, or cost-effectiveness assessments.

Agency officials we spoke with said a primary challenge of cost-benefit analysis is obtaining sufficient or quality data.[44] Some agency officials said that the data they needed were sometimes not available, while others said that available data lacked the quality or completeness necessary for their analyses. For example, when an agency is regulating a new product, data may not yet exist on the product's performance or effects on consumers. Officials from one agency that we spoke with also told us that sometimes data exist in a disaggregated manner, but that individual companies or industries are reluctant to share proprietary cost data. Agency officials said that they often use the notice and comment period to request data from the public or to seek input on the data the agency used in its analyses. However, some agency officials told us that while the comment process provides agencies with important information and perspectives that often lead to improvements in the final rules, the comment process generally does not result in obtaining complete data sets that agencies can use in their analyses. Agency officials said that they often received general comments that the agency's estimates are over- or understated, but that these comments generally lack supporting data that are complete enough for the agency to use in its own analysis—

---

[44]Our review of federal agencies' retrospective regulatory analysis practices also found agencies faced challenges with obtaining appropriate data. For more detail, see GAO-14-268. In addition, we have made recommendations in the past about the need for some agencies to plan for and collect data to perform regulatory analysis, such as when completing retrospective reviews of existing regulations. We continue to believe that such actions will help improve agency use of data throughout the rulemaking process. For examples of such recommendations, see GAO, *Dodd-Frank Act Regulations: Implementation Could Benefit from Additional Analyses and Coordination*, GAO-12-151 (Washington, D.C.: Nov. 10, 2011).

although one agency said that the public comment process periodically provides useful data which are incorporated into its cost-benefit analyses. Additionally, some agency officials said that if they are faced with a short statutory deadline for issuing a rule, they may decide not to collect some data because the process for receiving information collections approval (established by PRA) can sometimes be time consuming.[45]

When data, for whatever reason, were not available and agencies could not monetize all costs and benefits, they sometimes used other quantitative and qualitative information to evaluate rules. We found that between July 1, 2011, and June 30, 2013, executive agencies included some quantitative or qualitative measures of costs and benefits in all economically significant rules. Similarly, independent regulatory agencies provided quantitative or qualitative information on costs and benefits in almost every major rule issued in our time frame. For example, independent regulatory agencies did not include any discussion of costs or benefits in 3 percent and 8 percent of major rules, respectively.

We found a different situation for significant rules issued by executive agencies. We estimate that agencies did not include a discussion of costs in about 43 percent of significant rules and did not include a discussion of benefits in approximately 34 percent of significant rules.[46] Reasons for the omissions may include updating of a rule (listing of items in one rule to be consistent across other rules) or because the agency determined that the rule itself would not result in any specific costs or benefits. For example, when President Obama recognized South Sudan as a sovereign state, the Department of Commerce's Bureau of Industry and Security issued a rule adding South Sudan to the Export Administration Regulations Commerce Country Chart.[47] For information on the extent to which the rules issued between July 1, 2011, and June 30, 2013, included qualitatively discussed, quantified, and monetized costs and benefits, see appendix III.

---

[45]See note 12 *infra*.

[46]We also did not analyze the rules to gather information on whether inclusion of additional cost and benefit information would have promoted better decision making.

[47]76 Fed. Reg. 41,046 (July 13, 2011).

Agencies Included Alternatives More Often in Economically Significant and Major Rules Than in Significant Rules

Key Element: Alternatives

An analysis of alternatives allows agencies to decide on the best regulatory approach and achieve the maximum net benefits for society.

Source: GAO analysis of Executive Order 12866, *Circular A-4*, and general economic principles.

Evaluating net benefits of alternatives to a rule can provide decision makers and the public with useful information, even when economic efficiency is not the only or the overriding public policy objective of the rule. According to our analysis, executive agencies included a discussion of alternatives in about 81 percent of economically significant rules and in about 22 percent of significant rules.[48] Independent regulatory agencies included a discussion of alternatives in about 62 percent of their major rules.

Executive Order 12866's regulatory principles state that all rules should consider alternative regulatory actions, but it requires executive agencies to submit an analysis of alternatives to OIRA for review only for economically significant rules. According to the executive order and OMB guidance, agencies should consider a range of potentially effective and reasonably feasible regulatory alternatives, including the option of not regulating. Relevant alternatives might involve different approaches, with distinct advantages and disadvantages. For example, agencies can analyze alternatives with varying enforcement methods, degrees of stringency, compliance dates, or requirements based on firm size or geographic location. Agencies can also evaluate different regulatory approaches, such as performance standards rather than design standards, market-oriented approaches rather than direct controls, or informational measures rather than regulation. Alternatives we saw in our rule review included analyzing different computer model designs, alternate selection criteria for program participation, and varying levels of pollution abatement. While OMB guidance directs agencies to balance thoroughness and practicality when deciding on the appropriate number of alternatives to include and to consider reasonably feasible alternatives, in some instances feasible alternatives may not exist. For example, a rule amending the Federal Acquisition Regulation added Armenia to the list of countries that are members of the World Trade Organization Government Procurement Agreement (WTO GPA) as a result of a trade agreement.[49] The Department of Defense also issued a similar significant rule

---

[48]In our rule review, we did not count as alternatives the proposed rule or alternatives that were only part of the Regulatory Flexibility Act analyses. For alternatives proposed by commenters, we counted them only if the agency discussed how they analyzed and considered them.

[49]77 Fed. Reg. 12,935 (Mar. 2, 2012).

amending the Defense Federal Acquisition Regulation Supplement to include Armenia as a WTO GPA country.[50]

In our review of significant rules, we estimated that 38 percent of the rules that did not include a discussion of alternatives either had an underlying statute requiring the regulation which provided the agency with little or no discretion in the rulemaking process, or the rule included only minor or technical changes.[51] For example, the Office of Personnel Management issued a rule in direct response to changes made in the Department of Homeland Security Appropriations Act, 2008. (The Act provides early retirement and enhanced annuity benefits for customs and border protection officers employed by the Department of Homeland Security under certain federal employee retirement plans, among other provisions, and left little discretion to the agency in issuing the rule.[52]) In another example, the National Aeronautics and Space Administration issued a significant rule updating its procedures for handling allegations of research misconduct. The rule, which also did not include a discussion of alternatives, made non-substantive changes to policies and updated information to reflect organizational changes made at the agency.[53] We also observed five significant rules that added countries to specific lists of countries eligible to participate in certain trade activities as a result of treaties, international trade agreements, or presidential directives. As discussed previously, agency officials told us that at times statutes provide little or no discretion in their rulemaking—which can limit available feasible alternatives. Even if a statute leaves an agency little or no discretion in promulgating a rule, in some instances an agency may still include a discussion of alternatives—which could provide valuable information to agencies, Congress, and the public. For example, the National Marine Fisheries Service of the Department of Commerce's National Oceanic & Atmospheric Administration issued a rule to address shark conservation efforts as required by statute.[54] The agency analyzed the alternative of not regulating and stated that this option may

---

[50]77 Fed. Reg. 4631 (Jan. 30, 2012).

[51]Margin of error for this estimate is ±8 percentage points within a 95 percent confidence interval.

[52]76 Fed. Reg. 41,993 (July 18, 2011).

[53]77 Fed. Reg. 44,439 (July 30, 2012).

[54]78 Fed. Reg. 3338 (Jan. 16, 2013).

demonstrate the least burden or economic impact on small entities, but concluded that the agency did not have the discretion to not regulate. Because our rule review included only publicly available documentation, we do not know the extent to which agencies considered alternatives where there was no such discussion in the published rules. Furthermore, only economically significant regulatory actions have a requirement for agencies to submit such an analysis to OIRA. We also do not know the extent to which an inclusion of a discussion of alternatives would benefit decision making, especially in instances that involve statutory requirements or minor technical changes. For additional data from our rule review, see appendix III.

Agencies Used a Variety of Methods to Assess the Quality of Cost and Benefit Data and Generally Did Not Reevaluate Cost-Benefit Analyses after Implementing Rules

Agencies' Assessment Methods Depended on the Type and Use of Data

Our review of final rules found that agencies included a discussion of how they assessed the quality of data more often in economically significant rules than in significant or major rules. When conducting all regulatory analyses, including cost-benefit analyses, agencies are required by the Data Quality Act,[55] *Circular A-4*, and OMB data quality guidelines to use the best reasonably obtainable scientific, technical, and economic information available. The information should be based on peer-reviewed literature and when available, agencies should provide a source for all original information. Both independent and executive agency officials told us that they used one or more methods to assess the quality of data used in their cost-benefit analyses, but executive agency officials said the

---

[55]Pub. L. No. 106-554, § 515, 114 Stat. 2763, 2763A-153 (Dec. 21, 2000).

application of these methods depends on the type and use of the data. These methods include

- relying on the peer review process, particularly for science-driven data, to help ensure the data used in analyses are the most current and appropriate data available;
- consulting with expert panels, including academic and regulatory advisory committees, to discuss the usefulness and applicability of data the agency plans to use in its analyses;
- collecting and using data generated from internal and government-wide databases of information collected from the agencies' regulated entities;
- using techniques such as regularly reviewing data for outliers and triangulating data using multiple sources;
- routinely re-evaluating databases and the algorithms used for analysis; and
- requesting input from the public during the comment process.

Officials from executive and independent regulatory agencies told us they use significant resources for collecting, analyzing, and assessing the quality of the data used in rulemaking. For example (and as previously mentioned) agency officials told us that they have economists and other staff with expertise in cost-benefit analysis. At some agencies, officials said the chief economist plays a significant role in the regulatory cost-benefit analysis process. Agencies' use of contractors includes having them document and explain the quality of the underlying data. Agency officials also stated, and we observed in our review of rules, that they often acknowledge the limitations of their data in their cost-benefit analyses. Agency officials said they face many challenges in using data for cost-benefit analyses, but when the data are critical to the analyses that influence policy decisions, they commit more resources to obtaining data and to assessing their quality.

Three Agencies Provided Examples of Reevaluating Cost-Benefit Analyses, and Other Agencies Cited Reasons for Not Revisiting Their Analyses

Three of the seventeen agencies that we contacted provided examples of revisiting their cost-benefit analyses after rulemaking. These three agencies cited examples of reviewing implemented rules to compare cost outcomes to the estimates included in the original rule. The Nuclear Energy Institute performed a case study of three implemented Nuclear Regulatory Commission (NRC) rules in order to compare estimated to actual costs. The results of these case studies are that the estimated implementation costs were between two and nineteen times lower than actual implementation costs. The Nuclear Energy Institute submitted the case studies to NRC. NRC is considering using the results and recommendations provided in these case studies to improve NRC's regulatory analysis process. The Environmental Protection Agency (EPA) was required to conduct periodic scientifically-reviewed studies to assess the benefits and costs of the entire Clean Air Act. As of March 2014, EPA was evaluating twelve rules comparing key drivers of compliance costs to the original cost estimates. EPA officials told us that when completed, they intend to use information from these reviews to inform future cost-benefit analyses. A third agency—the Department of Labor—also told us that since 2000 it has done ten retrospective studies of major rules to improve their cost-benefit analyses. To the extent that appropriate data were readily available, these retrospective studies have examined the accuracy of benefits and cost estimates.

Consistent with principles in Executive Orders 12866 and 13563, agencies could obtain more information on the effectiveness of their cost-benefit analyses by revisiting cost-benefit estimates made during the rulemaking process after actual data become available. Having such information on effectiveness could in turn promote better decision making.[56] However, agencies said that they need to balance the resources needed to revisit their cost-benefit analyses with the benefits of potential information gained.

Officials from the other agencies we spoke with provided reasons for not re-evaluating their original cost-benefit analyses. Officials from a few agencies told us that a lack of resources—such as available time to conduct such analysis and access to sufficient and quality data—was the main reason for not conducting such reviews. One agency official said that in many situations, such reviews would not provide them with useful information for how they conduct their cost-benefit analyses given the rapidly changing environment in which they regulate. Agency officials also cited the difficulty in properly attributing actual costs and benefits to a particular rule in instances where several overlapping or sequential rules affect the regulated entity, or in instances where the regulated entities may have voluntarily adopted the provisions of the regulation even in the absence of the regulation.

[56]A reevaluation of cost-benefit analyses could also aid agencies in performing retrospective analyses, where agencies are directed by executive order to periodically review their existing significant regulations to determine whether they should be modified, streamlined, expanded, or repealed, so as to make the agency's regulatory program more effective or less burdensome. See GAO-14-268.

Conclusions

Federal agencies and OIRA could do more to improve the transparency of the rulemaking process. Our review of 109 significant rules showed that some agencies provided clear information about why some rules were deemed significant, but many did not. Publishing information regarding the reasons for designating a rule as significant would enhance transparency in the rulemaking process and would align with a key component of internal control requirements. Publication of this information would also reinforce the executive orders and guidance documents directing agencies to take specific steps to be more transparent in their decision-making and operations. In addition to such direction, executive orders contain criteria for how agencies should categorize their regulations as significant regulatory actions; publishing these reasons may contribute to a more consistent application of the criteria. Without information explaining the reason why rules are designated as significant, Congress, the public, and other federal agencies may have difficulty interpreting why some rules are significant and others are not. With this information, agencies' existing efforts to conduct regulatory cost-benefit analysis would be even more transparent and agencies would be able to better plan for future regulatory actions.

The usefulness of cost-benefit analysis for evaluating and informing decision makers and the public about the economic tradeoffs associated with proposed regulatory actions is well established. For both the executive agencies' economically significant rules and the independent regulatory agencies' major final rules that we reviewed, agencies included most of the selected key elements of cost-benefit analysis. For executive agencies' significant rules, agencies included selected key elements less often.

Recommendations for Executive Action

To improve transparency in the rulemaking process, provide agencies and the public with information on why regulations are considered to be significant regulatory actions, and promote consistency in the designation of rules as significant regulatory actions, we recommend that the Director of the Office of Management and Budget work with agencies to clearly communicate the reasons for designating a regulation as a significant regulatory action. Specifically, OMB should explain its reason for any changes to an agency's initial assessment of a regulation as non-significant. In addition, OMB should encourage agencies to clearly state in the preamble of final significant regulations the section of Executive Order 12866's definition of a significant regulatory action that applies to the regulation.

Agency Comments and Our Evaluation

We provided a draft of this report to the then Acting Director of the Office of Management and Budget, the Secretaries of Commerce, Defense, Education, Health and Human Services, the Interior, Labor, and Transportation, as well as the Administrators of the Environmental Protection Agency and the General Services Administration, the Chairs of the Commodity Futures Trading Commission, Federal Reserve Board, Nuclear Regulatory Commission, and the Securities and Exchange Commission; the Executive Director of the Consumer Product Safety Commission; the Managing Director of the Federal Communications Commission; the Director of the Consumer Financial Protection Bureau, and to the General Counsel of the National Labor Relations Board.

In oral comments received on August 22, 2014, staff from OMB's Office of Information and Regulatory Affairs discussed our findings, conclusions, and recommendations. The OMB staff did not state whether they agreed or disagreed with our recommendation. They said they engage in a dialogue with agency officials regarding significance determinations and generally agree with agencies' initial significance determinations for the vast majority of rules. They also said that they explain any disagreement regarding agencies' significance determinations to agency officials. They were not opposed to the language in our recommendation directing agencies to include the relevant portion of Executive Order 12866's definition of significant regulatory action in the preamble to rules. OMB staff also provided technical comments, which are incorporated into the report where appropriate.

In response to this discussion, we made minor revisions to the recommendation language to more accurately reflect the role of agency officials in establishing an initial significance determination along with OIRA's role in reviewing this determination. Although significance determinations are a shared responsibility, OIRA's role in reviewing agencies' determinations places responsibility for explaining the reason for a disagreement with OIRA. A shared understanding of the reason for a designation will promote increased transparency by allowing agencies to include this information in the rule.

We also received technical comments from the Departments of Health and Human Services, the Interior, and Labor, as well as from the Consumer Product Safety Commission, Environmental Protection Agency, Federal Communications Commission, Federal Reserve Board, General Services Administration, Nuclear Regulatory Commission, and Securities and Exchange Commission, which are incorporated into the report where appropriate.

We are sending copies of this report to the Director of the Office of Management and Budget, the Secretaries of Commerce, Defense, Education, Health and Human Services, the Interior, Labor, and Transportation, as well as the Administrators of the Environmental Protection Agency and the General Services Administration, the Chairs of the Commodity Futures Trading Commission, Federal Reserve Board, Nuclear Regulatory Commission, and the Securities and Exchange Commission; the Executive Director of the Consumer Product Safety Commission; the Managing Director of the Federal Communications Commission; the Director of the Consumer Financial Protection Bureau, and to the General Counsel of the National Labor Relations Board. We are also sending copies of this report to relevant congressional committees. In addition, this report is available at no charge on GAO's website at http://www.gao.gov.

If you or your staff have any questions about this report, please contact me at (202) 512-6806 or sagerm@gao.gov. Contact points for our Offices of Congressional Relations and Public Affairs may be found on the last page of this report. GAO staff who have made contributions to this report are listed in appendix V.

Sincerely,

Michelle Sager
Director, Strategic Issues

Appendix I: Objectives, Scope, and Methodology

This report addresses (1) how often and to what extent significant, economically significant, and major rules include key elements for assessing or analyzing benefits and costs; and (2) how and to what extent agencies assess the quality of the scientific, technical, and other types of data they use to consider costs and benefits. In order to assess how often and to what extent agencies included key elements for assessing and analyzing costs and benefits in federal regulations, we drew a generalizeable sample and reviewed a total of 203 final rules that were issued and published in the *Federal Register* between July 1, 2011, and June 30, 2013, to determine whether they contained what we define for the purposes of this report as key elements of a cost-benefit analysis: a discussion of the problem the rule intends to address; the identification (i.e., a qualitative discussion), quantification, or monetization of costs; the identification, quantification, or monetization of benefits; and a discussion of alternatives.[1] We drew our definition of key elements of a cost-benefit analysis from the Office of Management and Budget's (OMB) *Circular A-4*, Executive Order 12866, and general economic principles. *Circular A-4*, consistent with standard economic principles, identifies these selected elements as basic elements to include in the regulatory analysis that is required by Executive Order 12866 for economically significant rules. We also consider these basic elements important to any regulatory cost-benefit assessment and analysis. We recognize that there are other elements that would be viewed as key to include in a full and complete regulatory analysis, such as the identification of an economic baseline and discussion of uncertainties. The scope of this report is focused on the four selected key elements.

For significant and economically significant rules from executive agencies, we reviewed a stratified random sample (stratified by whether significant or economically significant) of final rules of both types issued within a 2-year period. To identify the full population of rules, on October 17, 2013, we downloaded a list of all final significant and economically significant rules published in the *Federal Register* between July 1, 2011, and June 30, 2013, from OMB's Office of Information and Regulatory Affairs' (OIRA) web site (www.reginfo.gov). Because OIRA can make updates to this list if errors are detected or rules are delayed in being added to the database, the list we downloaded is a snapshot of what was

---

[1]For the list of rules we reviewed as part of our sample, see app. II.

available on October 17, 2013. Table 3 summarizes our population,
sample, and final in-scope sample sizes by rule type.

**Table 3: Population, Selected Sample, and Final In-scope Sample Size for
Significant and Economically Significant Rules Issued between July 1, 2011 and
June 30, 2013**

Rule type	Population size	Selected sample	In-scope sample
Economically significant rules	78	57	55
Significant rules	284	117	111
Total	**362**	**174**	**166**

Source: GAO analysis of population of rules listed on www.reginfo.gov on October 17, 2013.| GAO-14-714.

Because we followed a probability procedure based on random
selections, our sample is only one of a large number of samples that we
might have drawn. Since each sample could have provided different
estimates, we express our confidence in the precision of our particular
sample's results as a 95 percent confidence interval. This is the interval
that would contain the actual population value for 95 percent of the
samples we could have drawn. Unless otherwise noted, all percentage
estimates in this report based on this sample have 95 percent confidence
intervals within ± 7 percentage points of the estimate.

While we determined that the reliability of the data we used from
www.reginfo.gov to be sufficient for the purposes of our review, we did
find some instances of inconsistent information which we corrected for
our analysis. After downloading the list of rules from www.reginfo.gov and
before selecting our sample, we excluded one rule from the population
because it appeared five times, once as a rule, and three times as a delay
of the rule's implementation date, and finally as an indefinite delay to rule
implementation. For the rules in our selected sample, we confirmed that
the rules had downloaded in the proper category of significant or
economically significant by reading the rules, confirming the date of
publication in the *Federal Register* to ensure the rules were within our
scope, and, for economically significant rules included in our analysis,
checking for major rules reports in the Congressional Review Act[2] (CRA)
database on www.gao.gov.

---

[2] 5 U.S.C. § 802(a)

In the course of our review, we identified eight rules as out of scope for
our analysis. These included two rules that were published outside the
time frame for our population, and four rules that were non-significant
regulatory actions. In addition, one rule was issued jointly under two
agencies, and another rule consisted of two separate identification
numbers; for each of these two rules the extraneous case was excluded
from our analysis. In addition to identifying these out of scope cases, we
found that two rules sampled from the significant rule stratum were
actually economically significant rules. In our analysis, these two rules are
included with the other economically significant rules in producing
estimates of that rule type. As a result of these adjustments, the final
sample we used for producing our estimates consisted of 109 significant
and 57 economically significant rules.

We also reviewed the population of all major rules issued by independent
regulatory agencies within the same time frame. We drew our list of major
rules from independent regulatory agencies from GAO's CRA database.
Under CRA, agencies are required to submit rules to Congress and GAO
before they can take effect. CRA requires GAO to report to Congress on
whether an agency, in promulgating a major rule, has complied with the
regulatory process. Because there were only 37 major rules issued within
the scope of our 2-year review period, we examined all of them. Values
reported for those rules are population values for that period and thus are
not subject to sampling error and are not estimates. We determined that
the data we used from the CRA database were reliable for the purposes
of our review of key elements of cost-benefit analyses.

To conduct the rule review, two reviewers independently analyzed and
coded the contents of the three types of rules to identify the presence of
key elements of cost-benefit analysis. The reviewers followed a code
book instructing them on how to apply our criteria for the presence or
absence of key elements to the rules. The reviewers reviewed the final
rules as published in the *Federal Register*. In instances where the rule did
not contain an element we were looking for, the reviewers also reviewed
documentation in the regulatory dockets, accessed through
www.regulations.gov. Such documentation included regulatory impact
analyses, proposed rules, or other supplemental information. A third party
examined the codes assigned by the reviewers to ensure that coding
criteria were consistently applied and resolved instances where the two
coders were not in agreement. In a few instances where this third party
review indicated a code may not have been applied in accordance with
coding criteria, a fourth party also reviewed the code. For significant rules
that we coded as not containing a discussion of alternatives, we further

reviewed the rules to determine how often these rules had little or no discretion in the rulemaking process or were making minor or technical changes. We recognize that agencies were not required to include all of the key elements for all of the rule types we reviewed and that it is not always feasible to include all key elements in a rule. For example, Executive Order 12866 does not require agencies to submit to OIRA an analysis of alternatives for rules that are not economically significant regulatory actions. Also, our analysis was not designed to evaluate the quality of the cost-benefit analysis in the rules; therefore, we did not conclude that the presence of all key elements indicated that the cost-benefit analysis provided information regarding the quality of the review and we did not conclude that the absence of a key element was necessarily a deficiency.

To supplement the rule review and to determine how and to what extent agencies assessed the quality of the data used in cost-benefit analyses, we conducted a series of roundtable discussions with officials from 17 of the 32 independent and executive branch agencies that issued the rules that we reviewed.[3] We chose the agencies to participate in our roundtable discussions based on how often their rules appeared in our sample. For independent regulatory agencies, we invited the eight agencies that issued major rules during the period we reviewed to participate in the roundtable discussions.[4] For executive agencies, we invited the six agencies that had the largest number of significant rules in our sample and the six agencies that had the largest number of economically

---

[3]The following agencies participated in our roundtable discussions: Commodity Futures Trading Commission, Consumer Financial Protection Bureau, Consumer Product Safety Commission, Department of Commerce, Department of Defense, Department of Education, Department of Health and Human Services, Department of Labor, Department of Transportation, Environmental Protection Agency, Federal Communications Commission, Federal Reserve System, General Services Administration, National Labor Relations Board, Nuclear Regulatory Commission, and the Securities and Exchange Commission. The Federal Acquisition Regulation (FAR) is issued jointly by the General Services Administration (GSA), Department of Defense, and the National Aeronautics and Space Administration. GSA participated in the roundtables to discuss the FAR, and did not discuss rules issued solely by GSA. The Department of Defense participants discussed both FAR and other defense regulations. The Department of the Interior chose to have an individual interview with us in lieu of participating in the roundtable discussions.

[4]The National Labor Relations Board (NLRB) had one major rule issued within our timeframe that was later withdrawn. We invited officials from NLRB to participate to discuss their experience with the process of issuing that major rule. NLRB is included in the count of eight independent regulatory agencies that participated in our roundtables.

significant rules in our sample. Three agencies appeared on both lists, resulting in a total of nine executive branch agencies attending our roundtables. We conducted four roundtable sessions: two included independent regulatory agencies and two included executive agencies. We also met with one agency individually. At these roundtables, we asked agency officials who were involved in the development of agency regulations to discuss their interactions with OIRA, challenges they face in including the key elements of cost-benefit analyses, steps they take to assess the quality of their data, and how often, if at all, they compare estimated costs and benefits in rules to outcome data after rule implementation. For the executive agency roundtables, we also asked agency officials to compare their approaches to cost-benefit analyses in significant and economically significant rules.

We conducted this performance audit from June 2013 to September 2014 in accordance with generally accepted government auditing standards. Those standards require that we plan and perform the audit to obtain sufficient, appropriate evidence to provide a reasonable basis for our findings and conclusions based on our audit objectives. We believe that the evidence obtained provides a reasonable basis for our findings and conclusions based on our audit objectives.

Appendix II: List of Rules Issued between July 1, 2011 and June 30, 2013 Included in Review Sample

Table 4: Economically Significant Rules

Title	Rule identification number	*Federal Register* number	Responsible agency
Air Cargo Screening	1652-AA64	76 Fed. Reg. 51,848	DHS
Provisional Unlawful Presence Waivers of Inadmissibility for Certain Immediate Relatives	1615-AB99	78 Fed. Reg. 536	DHS
Setting and Adjusting Patent Fees	0651-AC54	78 Fed. Reg. 4212	DOC
Energy Efficiency Standards for Fluorescent Lamp Ballasts	1904-AB50	76 Fed. Reg. 70,548	DOE
Energy Efficiency for Dishwashers	1904-AC64	77 Fed. Reg. 31,918	DOE
Energy Conservation Standards for Residential Clothes Washers	1904-AB90	77 Fed. Reg. 59,719	DOE
Energy Efficiency Standards for Microwave Ovens (Standby and Off Mode)	1904-AC07	78 Fed. Reg. 36,316	DOE
Migratory Bird Hunting; 2011-12 Migratory Game Bird Hunting Regulations	1018-AX34	76 Fed. Reg. 58,682	DOI
Migratory Bird Hunting; 2011-12 Migratory Game Bird Hunting Regulations	1018-AX34	76 Fed. Reg. 59,271	DOI
Increased Safety Measures for Oil and Gas Operations on the Outer Continental Shelf (OCS)	1014-AA02	77 Fed. Reg. 50,856	DOI
Migratory Bird Hunting; 2012-2013 Migratory Game Bird Hunting Regulations	1018-AX97	77 Fed. Reg. 58,444	DOI
Migratory Bird Hunting; 2012-2013 Migratory Game Bird Hunting Regulations	1018-AX97	77 Fed. Reg. 58,628	DOI
James Zadroga 9/11 Health and Compensation Act of 2010	1105-AB39	76 Fed. Reg. 54,112	DOJ
Statutory Exemption for Provision of Investment Advice	1210-AB35	76 Fed. Reg. 66,136	DOL
Improved Fee Disclosure for Pension Plans	1210-AB08	77 Fed. Reg. 5632	DOL
Labor Certification Process and Enforcement for Temporary Employment in Occupations Other Than Agriculture or Registered Nursing in the United States (H-2B Workers)	1205-AB58	77 Fed. Reg. 10,038	DOL
Hazard Communication	1218-AC20	77 Fed. Reg. 17,574	DOL
Commercial Medium- and Heavy-Duty On-Highway Vehicles and Work Truck Fuel Efficiency Standards	2127-AK74	76 Fed. Reg. 57,106	DOT
National Registry of Certified Medical Examiners	2126-AA97	77 Fed. Reg. 24,104	DOT
Positive Train Control Systems Amendments (RRR)	2130-AC27	77 Fed. Reg. 28,285	DOT
Major Capital Investment Projects (RRR)	2132-AB02	78 Fed. Reg. 1992	DOT
Race to the Top Fund Phase 3	1894-AA01	76 Fed. Reg. 70,986	EDUCATION
Teacher Incentive Fund	1810-AB12	77 Fed. Reg. 35,758	EDUCATION
Race to the Top—Early Learning Challenge Phase 2	1810-AB15	77 Fed. Reg. 58,301	EDUCATION
Federal Perkins Loan Program, Federal Family Education Loan Program, and William D. Ford Federal Direct Loan Program	1840-AD05	77 Fed. Reg. 66,088	EDUCATION
Transport Rule (CAIR Replacement Rule)	2060-AP50	76 Fed. Reg. 48,208	EPA
Supplemental Notice for Transport Rule (CAIR Replacement Rule)	2060-AR01	76 Fed. Reg. 80,760	EPA

Title	Rule identification number	*Federal Register* number	Responsible agency
National Emission Standards for Hazardous Air Pollutants From Coal- and Oil-Fired Electric Utility Steam Generating Units and Standards of Performance for Electric Utility Steam Generating Units	2060-AP52	77 Fed. Reg. 9304	EPA
Joint Rulemaking to Establish 2017 and Later Model Year Light Duty Vehicle GHG Emissions and CAFE Standards	2060-AQ54	77 Fed. Reg. 62,624	EPA
Review of the National Ambient Air Quality Standards for Particulate Matter	2060-AO47	78 Fed. Reg. 3086	EPA
Reconsideration of Final National Emission Standards for Hazardous Air Pollutants for Reciprocating Internal Combustion Engines	2060-AQ58	78 Fed. Reg. 6674	EPA
Prospective Payment System and Consolidated Billing for Skilled Nursing Facilities—Update for FY 2012 (CMS-1351-F)	0938-AQ29	76 Fed. Reg. 48,486	HHS
Proposed Changes to the Hospital Inpatient Prospective Payment Systems for Acute Care Hospitals and FY 2012 Rates and to the Long-Term Care Hospital PPS and FY 2012 Rates (CMS-1518-F)	0938-AQ24	76 Fed. Reg. 51,476	HHS
Medicaid Recovery Audit Contractors (CMS-6034-F)	0938-AQ19	76 Fed. Reg. 57,808	HHS
Medicare Shared Savings Program: Accountable Care Organizations (CMS-1345-F)	0938-AQ22	76 Fed. Reg. 67,802	HHS
End-Stage Renal Disease Prospective Payment System for CY 2012, Quality Incentive Program for PY 2013 and PY 2014; Ambulance Fee Schedule; and Durable Medical Equipment (CMS-1577-F)	0938-AQ27	76 Fed. Reg. 70,228	HHS
Revisions to Payment Policies Under the Physician Fee Schedule and Part B for CY 2012 (CMS-1524-FC)	0938-AQ25	76 Fed. Reg. 73,026	HHS
Changes to the Hospital Outpatient Prospective Payment System and Ambulatory Surgical Center Payment System for CY 2012 (CMS-1525-FC)	0938-AQ26	76 Fed. Reg. 74,122	HHS
Policy and Technical Changes to the Medicare Advantage and the Medicare Prescription Drug Benefit Programs for Contract Year 2013 (CMS-4157-FC)	0938-AQ86	77 Fed. Reg. 22,072	HHS
Changes in Provider and Supplier Enrollment, Ordering and Referring, and Documentation Requirements; and Changes in Provider Agreements (CMS-6010-F)	0938-AQ01	77 Fed. Reg. 25,284	HHS
Community First Choice Option (CMS-2337-F)	0938-AQ35	77 Fed. Reg. 26,828	HHS
Medicare and Medicaid Programs: Reform of Hospital and Critical Access Hospital Conditions of Participation (CMS-3244-F)	0938-AQ89	77 Fed. Reg. 29,034	HHS
Prospective Payment System and Consolidated Billing for Skilled Nursing Facilities—Update for FY 2013 (CMS-1432-N)	0938-AR20	77 Fed. Reg. 46,214	HHS
Changes to the Hospital Inpatient and Long-Term Care Prospective Payment Systems for FY 2013 (CMS-1588-F)	0938-AR12	77 Fed. Reg. 53,258	HHS
Medicare and Medicaid Electronic Health Record Incentive Program—Stage 2 (CMS-0044-F)	0938-AQ84	77 Fed. Reg. 53,968	HHS
Administrative Simplification: Standard Unique Identifier for Health Plans and ICD-10 Compliance Date Delay (CMS-0040-F)	0938-AQ13	77 Fed. Reg. 54,664	HHS

Title	Rule identification number	*Federal Register* number	Responsible agency
Payments for Services Furnished by Certain Primary Care Physicians and Charges for Vaccine Administration Under the Vaccines for Children Program (CMS-2370-F)	0938-AQ63	77 Fed. Reg. 66,670	HHS
Changes to the End-Stage Renal Disease Prospective Payment System for CY 2013 (CMS-1352-F)	0938-AR13	77 Fed. Reg. 67,450	HHS
Proposed Changes to Hospital OPPS and CY 2013 Payment Rates; ASC Payment System and CY 2013 Payment Rates (CMS-1589-FC)	0938-AR10	77 Fed. Reg. 68,210	HHS
Modifications to the HIPAA Privacy, Security, Enforcement, and Breach Notification Rules	0945-AA03	78 Fed. Reg. 5566	HHS
Patient Protection and Affordable Care Act; Health Insurance Market: Rate Review (CMS-9972-F)	0938-AR40	78 Fed. Reg. 13,406	HHS
Notice of Benefit and Payment Parameters (CMS-9964-F)	0938-AR51	78 Fed. Reg. 15,410	HHS
Multi-State Exchanges; Implementations for Affordable Care Act Provisions	3206-AM47	78 Fed. Reg. 15,560	OPM
Assessment of Fees for Large Bank Holding Companies and Nonbank Financial Companies Supervised by the Federal Reserve to Cover the Expenses of the Financial Research Fund	1505-AC42	77 Fed. Reg. 29,884	TREASURY
Nutrition Standards in the National School Lunch and School Breakfast Programs	0584-AD59	77 Fed. Reg. 4088	USDA
Rural Broadband Access Loans and Loan Guarantees	0572-AC06	78 Fed. Reg. 8353	USDA
Vocational Rehabilitation and Employment Program—Changes to Subsistence Allowance	2900-AO10	77 Fed. Reg. 1872	VA

Source: GAO review of regulations from the *Federal Register*. | GAO-14-714

Table 5: Significant Rules

Title	Rule identification number	*Federal Register* number	Responsible agency
Partner Vetting In USAID Acquisitions	0412-AA63	77 Fed. Reg. 8166	AID
Establishment of Global Entry Program	1651-AA73	77 Fed. Reg. 5681	DHS
Exports and Reexports to the Newly Established State of the Republic of South Sudan	0694-AF27	76 Fed. Reg. 41,046	DOC
Changes to Implement the Prioritized Examination Track (Track I) of the Enhanced Examination Timing Control Procedures	0651-AC62	76 Fed. Reg. 59,050	DOC
Exports and Reexports to Liechtenstein	0694-AF33	76 Fed. Reg. 70,337	DOC
Export and Reexport License Requirements for Certain Microwave and Millimeter Wave Electronic Components	0694-AF38	77 Fed. Reg. 1017	DOC
Revision of Critical Habitat Designation for the Endangered Leatherback Sea Turtle	0648-AX06	77 Fed. Reg. 4170	DOC
Foreign-Trade Zones in the United States	0625-AA81	77 Fed. Reg. 12,112	DOC

Title	Rule identification number	*Federal Register* number	Responsible agency
Revisions to the Export Administration Regulations (EAR): Export Control Classification Number 0Y521 Series, Items Not Otherwise Listed on the Commerce Control List (CCL)	0694-AF17	77 Fed. Reg. 22,191	DOC
Changes to Implement the Supplemental Examination Provisions of the Leahy-Smith America Invents Act and to Revise Reexamination Fees	0651-AC69	77 Fed. Reg. 48,828	DOC
High Seas Driftnet Fishing Moratorium Protection Act; Identification and Certification Procedures to Address Shark Conservation	0648-BA89	78 Fed. Reg. 3338	DOC
Revisions to the Export Administration Regulations: Implementation of Export Control Reform; Retrospective Regulatory Review	0694-AF65	78 Fed. Reg. 22,660	DOC
Framework Adjustment 50 to the Northeast Multispecies Fishery Management Plan	0648-BC97	78 Fed. Reg. 26,172	DOC
TRICARE; Inclusion of Retail Network Pharmacies as Authorized TRICARE Providers for the Administration of TRICARE Covered Vaccines	0720-AB37	76 Fed. Reg. 41,063	DOD
Administering Trafficking in Persons Regulations (DFARS Case 2011-D051)	0750-AH41	76 Fed. Reg. 71,830	DOD
New Designated Country-Armenia (DFARS Case 2011-D057)	0750-AH48	77 Fed. Reg. 4631	DOD
Independent Research and Development Technical Descriptions (DFARS Case 2010-D011)	0750-AG96	77 Fed. Reg. 4632	DOD
Issuing and Reissuing Nationwide Permits	0710-AA71	77 Fed. Reg. 10,184	DOD
Business Systems—Definition and Administration (DFARS Case 2009-D038)	0750-AG58	77 Fed. Reg. 11,355	DOD
Commercial Determination Approval (DFARS Case 2011-D041)	0750-AH61	77 Fed. Reg. 14,480	DOD
Contractors Performing Private Security Functions (DFARS Case 2011-D023)	0750-AH28	77 Fed. Reg. 35,883	DOD
DoD Unclassified Controlled Nuclear Information (UCNI)	0790-AI64	77 Fed. Reg. 43,506	DOD
Only One Offer (DFARS Case 2011-D013)	0750-AH11	78 Fed. Reg. 39,126	DOD
Updating State Residential Building Energy Efficiency Codes	1904-AC17	76 Fed. Reg. 42,688	DOE
Determination Regarding Energy Efficiency Standard for Buildings, ANSI/ASHRAE/IESNA Standard 90.1-2007	1904-AC18	76 Fed. Reg. 43,287	DOE
Residential, Business, and Wind and Solar Resource Leases on Indian Land	1070-AE73	77 Fed. Reg. 72,440	DOI
Endangered and Threatened Wildlife and Plants; Revising the Critical Habitat Designation for the Southwestern Willow Flycatcher	1018-AX43	78 Fed. Reg. 344	DOI
Revisions to Safety and Environmental Management Systems Requirements (SEMS)	1014-AA04	78 Fed. Reg. 20,423	DOI
Implementation of the Methamphetamine Production Prevention Act of 2008	1117-AB25	76 Fed. Reg. 74,696	DOJ
Nondiscrimination on the Basis of Disability by Public Accommodations and in Commercial Facilities; Swimming Pools	1190-AA68	77 Fed. Reg. 16,163	DOJ

Title	Rule identification number	*Federal Register* number	Responsible agency
Delaying the Compliance Date for Certain Requirements of the Regulations Implementing Titles II and III of the Americans with Disabilities Act	1190-AA69	77 Fed. Reg. 30,174	DOJ
Consolidation of Seizure and Forfeiture Regulations	1105-AA74	77 Fed. Reg. 56,093	DOJ
Application Procedures and Criteria for Approval of Nonprofit Budget and Credit Counseling Agencies by U.S. Trustees	1105-AB17	78 Fed. Reg. 16,138	DOJ
Application Procedures and Criteria for Approval of Providers of a Personal Financial Management Instructional Course by United States Trustees	1105-AB31	78 Fed. Reg. 16,159	DOJ
YouthBuild Program Regulation	1205-AB49	77 Fed. Reg. 9112	DOL
Examination of Work Areas in Underground Coal Mines for Violations of Mandatory Health or Safety Standards	1219-AB75	77 Fed. Reg. 20,700	DOL
Pattern of Violations	1219-AB73	78 Fed. Reg. 5056	DOL
Filings Required of Multiple Employer Welfare Arrangements and Certain Other Entities That Offer or Provide Coverage for Medical Care to the Employees of Two or More Employers	1210-AB51	78 Fed. Reg. 13,781	DOL
Vehicle Labeling—Fuel Economy, Greenhouse Gas, and Other Emissions	2127-AK73	76 Fed. Reg. 39,478	DOT
Part 121 — Activation of Ice Protection	2120-AJ43	76 Fed. Reg. 52,241	DOT
Flight and Duty Time Limitations and Rest Requirements	2120-AJ58	77 Fed. Reg. 330	DOT
National Standards for Traffic Control Devices; the Manual on Uniform Traffic Control Devices for Streets and Highways; Revision	2125-AF43	77 Fed. Reg. 28,460	DOT
Inspection, Repair, and Maintenance; Driver-Vehicle Inspection Report for Intermodal Equipment	2126-AB34	77 Fed. Reg. 34,846	DOT
Requiring the Use of the New York North Shore Route for Helicopters	2120-AJ75	77 Fed. Reg. 39,911	DOT
Environmental Impact and Related Procedures	2132-AB03	78 Fed. Reg. 8964	DOT
Corrections and Minor Revisions to the MY 2014-2018 Greenhouse Gas Emissions Standards and Fuel Efficiency Standards for Medium- and Heavy-Duty Engines and Vehicles	2127-AL31	78 Fed. Reg. 36,370	DOT
State Fiscal Stabilization Fund Program	1894-AA03	77 Fed. Reg. 4674	EDUCATION
Comprehensive Centers Program	1810-AB14	77 Fed. Reg. 33,574	EDUCATION
Disparate Impact and Reasonable Factors Other Than Age Under the Age Discrimination in Employment Act	3046-AA76	77 Fed. Reg. 19,080	EEOC
Lead; Clearance and Clearance Testing Requirements for the Renovation, Repair, and Painting Program	2070-AJ57	76 Fed. Reg. 47,918	EPA
TSCA Inventory Update Reporting Modifications	2070-AJ43	76 Fed. Reg. 50,816	EPA
Review of the National Ambient Air Quality Standards for Carbon Monoxide	2060-AI43	76 Fed. Reg. 54,294	EPA
NESHAP for Primary Lead Smelting	2060-AQ43	76 Fed. Reg. 70,834	EPA
Regulation of Fuels and Fuel Additives: 2012 Renewable Fuel Standards	2060-AQ76	77 Fed. Reg. 1320	EPA

Title	Rule identification number	*Federal Register* number	Responsible agency
Regulation To Establish No Discharge Zone in California State Waters Under CWA 312(f)(4)(A)	2009-AA04	77 Fed. Reg. 11,401	EPA
Widespread Use for Onboard Refueling Vapor Recovery and Stage II Waiver	2060-AQ97	77 Fed. Reg. 28,772	EPA
Effluent Limitations Guidelines and Standards for Airport Deicing Operations	2040-AE69	77 Fed. Reg. 29,168	EPA
Adoption of International NOx Standard for Aircraft Engines	2060-AO70	77 Fed. Reg. 36,342	EPA
Commercial and Industrial Solid Waste Incineration Units: Reconsideration and Final Amendments; Non-Hazardous Secondary Materials That Are Solid Waste	2060-AR15	78 Fed. Reg. 9112	EPA
National Emission Standard for Hazardous Air Pollutants for the Portland Cement Manufacturing Industry and Standards of Performance for Portland Cement Plants	2060-AQ93	78 Fed. Reg. 10,006	EPA
Regulation of Fuels and Fuel Additives: Identification of Additional Qualifying Renewable Fuel Pathways Under the Renewable Fuel Standard Program	2060-AR07	78 Fed. Reg. 14,190	EPA
National Emission Standards for Hazardous Air Pollutants: Coal- and Oil-Fired Electric Utility Steam Generating Units	2060-AR62	78 Fed. Reg. 24,073	EPA
National Emission Standards for Hazardous Air Pollutants (NESHAP) for Petroleum Refineries—Heat Exchanger Reconsideration	2060-AP84	78 Fed. Reg. 37,133	EPA
Risk and Technology Review for National Emission Standards for Hazardous Air Pollutants From the Pulp and Paper Industry	2060-AQ41	78 Fed. Reg. 55,698	EPA
FAR Case 2009-007, Equal Opportunity for Veterans	9000-AL67	76 Fed. Reg. 39,233	FAR
FAR Case 2008-025, Preventing Personal Conflicts of Interest for Contractor Employees Performing Acquisition Functions	9000-AL46	76 Fed. Reg. 68,017	FAR
FAR Case 2009-041, Sudan Waiver Process	9000-AL65	76 Fed. Reg. 68,037	FAR
FAR Case 2009-043, Time-and-Materials (T&M) and Labor-Hour (LH) Contracts for Commercial Items	9000-AL74	77 Fed. Reg. 194	FAR
FAR Case 2010-016, Public Access to the Federal Awardee Performance and Integrity Information System	9000-AL94	77 Fed. Reg. 197	FAR
FAR Case 2011-030, New Designated Country (Armenia) and Other Trade Agreements Updates	9000-AM16	77 Fed. Reg. 12,935	FAR
FAR Case 2010-009, Government Property	9000-AL95	77 Fed. Reg. 12,937	FAR
FAR Case 2008-039, Reporting Executive Compensation and First-Tier Subcontract Awards	9000-AL66	77 Fed. Reg. 44,047	FAR
Designation Renewal of Head Start Grantees	0970-AC44	76 Fed. Reg. 70,010	HHS
Revisions to Certain Durable Medical Equipment, Prosthetics, Orthotics and Supplies (DMEPOS) Suppliers Safeguards (CMS-6036-F2)	0938-AQ57	77 Fed. Reg. 14,989	HHS
Medical Loss Ratio Requirements under the Affordable Care Act—Notice Requirements (CMS-9998-F)	0938-AR41	77 Fed. Reg. 28,790	HHS
Home Health Prospective Payment System Rate for CY 2013 (CMS-1358-F)	0938-AR18	77 Fed. Reg. 67,068	HHS

Appendix II: List of Rules Issued between July
1, 2011 and June 30, 2013 Included in Review
Sample

Title	Rule identification number	*Federal Register* number	Responsible agency
Summary of Benefits and Coverage and Uniform Glossary	0938-AQ73	77 Fed. Reg. 8668	HHS
Establishment of Exchanges and Qualified Health Plans; Small Business Health Options Program (SHOP) (CMS-9964-F2)	0938-AR76	78 Fed. Reg. 33,233	HHS
Health Information Technology: New and Revised Standards, Implementation Specifications, and Certification Criteria for Electronic Health Record Technology	0991-AB82	78 Fed. Reg. 54,163	HHS
World Trade Center Health Program; Addition of Certain Types of Cancer to the List of WTC-Related Health Conditions	0920-AA49	77 Fed. Reg. 56,138	HHS
Federal Housing Administration (FHA) Single Family Lender Insurance Process: Eligibility, Indemnification, and Termination	2502-AI58	77 Fed. Reg. 3598	HUD
Equal Access to Housing in HUD Programs—Regardless of Sexual Orientation or Gender Identity (FR-5359)	2501-AD49	77 Fed. Reg. 5662	HUD
Federal Housing Administration (FHA): Hospital Mortgage Insurance Program—Refinancing Hospital Loans (FR-5334)	2502-AI74	78 Fed. Reg. 8330	HUD
Implementation of the Fair Housing Act's Discriminatory Effects Standard	2529-AA96	78 Fed. Reg. 11,460	HUD
Research Misconduct	2700-AD84	77 Fed. Reg. 44,439	NASA
Government Employees Serving in Official Capacity in Nonprofit Organizations; Sector Unit Investment Trusts	3209-AA09	78 Fed. Reg. 14,437	OGE
Retirement Eligibility for Customs and Border Protection Officers Under CSRS and FERS	3206-AL69	76 Fed. Reg. 41,993	OPM
Federal Employees Health Benefits Program; Community-Rated Health Plans	3206-AM39	77 Fed. Reg. 19,522	OPM
Noncompetitive Appointment of Certain Former Overseas Employees	3206-AM35	77 Fed. Reg. 42,902	OPM
Small Business Investment Companies—Energy Saving Qualified Investments	3245-AF86	77 Fed. Reg. 23,373	SBA
Small Business Size Standards; Administrative and Support, Waste Management and Remediation Services	3245-AG27	77 Fed. Reg. 72,691	SBA
Small Business Size Standards; Information	3245-AG26	77 Fed. Reg. 72,702	SBA
Small Business Jobs Act: Small Business Size and Status Integrity	3245-AG23	78 Fed. Reg. 38,811	SBA
Amendments to Regulations Regarding Major Life-Changing Events Affecting Income-Related Monthly Adjustment Amounts to Medicare Part B Premiums (3574F)	0960-AH06	76 Fed. Reg. 38,552	SSA
Electronic Substitutions for Form SSA-538	0960-AH02	76 Fed. Reg. 41,685	SSA
Protecting the Public and our Employees in Our Hearing Process	0960-AH29	77 Fed. Reg. 10,657	SSA
Revised Medical Criteria for Evaluating Visual Disorders	0960-AH28	78 Fed. Reg. 18,837	SSA
Amendment to the International Traffic in Arms Regulations: Temporary Export Exemption for Chemical Agent Protective Gear	1400-AC71	77 Fed. Reg. 25,865	STATE
Amendment to the International Traffic in Arms Regulations: Afghanistan	1400-AD26	77 Fed. Reg. 76,864	STATE
Amendment to the International Traffic in Arms Regulations: Initial Implementation of Export Control Reform	1400-AD37	78 Fed. Reg. 22,740	STATE

Title	Rule identification number	*Federal Register* number	Responsible agency
Comprehensive Iran Sanctions, Accountability, and Divestment Act of 2010 ("CISADA") Reporting Requirements Under Section 104(e)	1506-AB12	76 Fed. Reg. 62,607	TREASURY
Financial Crimes Enforcement Network: Anti-Money Laundering Program and Suspicious Activity Report Requirements for Non-Bank Residential Mortgage Lenders and Originators	1506-AB02	77 Fed. Reg. 8148	TREASURY
Application, Review, and Reporting for Waivers for State Innovation	1505-AC30	77 Fed. Reg. 11,700	TREASURY
Garnishment of Accounts Containing Federal Benefit Payments	1505-AC20	78 Fed. Reg. 32,099	TREASURY
Commercial Transportation of Equines to Slaughter	0579-AC49	76 Fed. Reg. 55,213	USDA
Chronic Wasting Disease in Elk and Deer; Interstate Movement Restrictions and Payment of Indemnity	0579-AB35	77 Fed. Reg. 35,542	USDA
Submission of Itineraries	0579-AD03	77 Fed. Reg. 76,809	USDA
Handling of Animals; Contingency Plans	0579-AC69	77 Fed. Reg. 76,815	USDA
Drug and Product Promotion by Pharmaceutical Company Representatives at VA Facilities	2900-AN42	77 Fed. Reg. 12,997	VA

Source: GAO review of regulations from the *Federal Register*. | GAO-14-714

Table 6: Major Rules

Title	Rule identification number	*Federal Register* number	Responsible agency
Bureau Of Consumer Financial Protection: Fair Credit Reporting (Regulation V)	3170-AA06	76 Fed. Reg. 79,308	CFPB
Bureau Of Consumer Financial Protection: Electronic Fund Transfers (Regulation E)	3170–AA15	77 Fed. Reg. 6194	CFPB
Bureau Of Consumer Financial Protection: Ability-To-Repay And Qualified Mortgage Standards Under The Truth In Lending Act (Regulation Z)	3170-AA17	78 Fed. Reg. 6408	CFPB
Bureau Of Consumer Financial Protection: Mortgage Servicing Rules Under The Real Estate Settlement Procedures Act (Regulation X)	3170–AA14	78 Fed. Reg. 10,696	CFPB
Bureau Of Consumer Financial Protection: Mortgage Servicing Rules Under The Truth In Lending Act (Regulation Z)	3170–AA14	78 Fed. Reg. 10,902	CFPB
Bureau Of Consumer Financial Protection: Loan Originator Compensation Requirements Under The Truth In Lending Act (Regulation Z)	3170-AA13	70 Fed. Reg. 11,200	CFPB
Commodity Futures Trading Commission: Whistleblower Incentives And Protection	3038-AD04	76 Fed. Reg. 53,172	CFTC
Commodity Futures Trading Commission: Swap Data Repositories: Registration Standards, Duties And Core Principles	3038-AD20	76 Fed. Reg. 54,538	CFTC
Commodity Futures Trading Commission: Derivatives Clearing Organization General Provisions And Core Principles	3038-AC98	76 Fed. Reg. 69,334	CFTC
Commodity Futures Trading Commission: Position Limits For Futures And Swaps	3038-AD17	76 Fed. Reg. 71,626	CFTC

Title	Rule identification number	*Federal Register* number	Responsible agency
Commodity Futures Trading Commission: Investment Of Customer Funds And Funds Held In An Account For Foreign Futures And Foreign Options Transactions	3038-AC79	76 Fed. Reg. 78,776	CFTC
Commodity Futures Trading Commission: Real-Time Public Reporting Of Swap Transaction Data	3038–AD08	77 Fed. Reg. 1182	CFTC
Commodity Futures Trading Commission: Swap Data Recordkeeping And Reporting Requirements	3038-AD19	77 Fed. Reg. 2136	CFTC
Commodity Futures Trading Commission: Protection Of Cleared Swaps Customer Contracts And Collateral; Conforming Amendments To The Commodity Broker Bankruptcy Provisions	3038-AC99	77 Fed. Reg. 6336	CFTC
Commodity Futures Trading Commission: Business Conduct Standards For Swap Dealers And Major Swap Participants With Counterparties	3038-AD25	77 Fed. Reg. 9734	CFTC
Commodity Futures Trading Commission: Swap Dealer And Major Swap Participant Recordkeeping, Reporting, And Duties Rules; Futures Commission Merchant And Introducing Broker Conflicts Of Interest Rules; And Chief Compliance Officer Rules For Swap Dealers, Major Swap Participants, And Futures Commission Merchants	3038-AC96	77 Fed. Reg. 20,128	CFTC
Commodity Futures Trading Commission: Customer Clearing Documentation, Timing Of Acceptance For Clearing, And Clearing Member Risk Management	3038-0092	77 Fed. Reg. 21,278	CFTC
Commodity Futures Trading Commission And Securities Exchange Commission: Further Definition Of "Swap Dealer," "Security-Based Swap Dealer," "Major Swap Participant," "Major Security-Based Swap Participant" And "Eligible Contract Participant"	3038-AD06	77 Fed. Reg. 30,596	CFTC
Commodity Futures Trading Commission: Core Principles And Other Requirements For Designated Contract Markets	3038-AD09	77 Fed. Reg. 36,612	CFTC
Further Definition Of "Swap," "Security-Based Swap," And "Security-Based Swap Agreement"; Mixed Swaps; Security-Based Swap Agreement Recordkeeping	3038-AD46	77 Fed. Reg. 48,208	CFTC
Commodity Futures Trading Commission: Clearing Exemption For Swaps Between Certain Affiliated Entities	3038- AD47	78 Fed. Reg. 21,750	CFTC
Commodity Futures Trading Commission: Core Principles And Other Requirements For Swap Execution Facilities	3038- AD18	78 Fed. Reg. 33,476	CFTC
Consumer Product Safety Commission: Testing And Labeling Pertaining To Product Certification	No RIN	76 Fed. Reg. 69,482	CPSC
Federal Communications Commission: Special Access For Price Cap Local Exchange Carriers; AT&T Corporation Petition For Rulemaking To Reform Regulation Of Incumbent Local Exchange Carrier Rates For Interstate Special Access Services	No RIN	78 Fed. Reg. 2572	FCC
Federal Reserve System: Debit Card Interchange Fees And Routing	7100-AD63	76 Fed. Reg. 43,394	FRS
Federal Reserve System: Debit Card Interchange Fees And Routing	7100-AD63	76 Fed. Reg. 43,478	FRS
National Labor Relations Board: Notification Of Employee Rights Under The National Labor Relations Act	3142- AA07	76 Fed. Reg. 54,006	NLRB

Title	Rule identification number	*Federal Register* number	Responsible agency
Nuclear Regulatory Commission: Revision Of Fee Schedules; Fee Recovery For Fiscal Year 2012	3150-AJ03	77 Fed. Reg. 35,809	NRC
Nuclear Regulatory Commission; Physical Protection Of Byproduct Material	3150-AI12	78 Fed. Reg. 16,922	NRC
Securities And Exchange Commission: Rules Implementing Amendments To The Investment Advisers Act Of 1940	3235-AK82	76 Fed. Reg. 42,950	SEC
Securities And Exchange Commission: Large Trader Reporting	3235-AK55	76 Fed. Reg. 46,960	SEC
Commodity Futures Trading Commission And Securities And Exchange Commission: Reporting By Investment Advisers To Private Funds And Certain Commodity Pool Operators And Commodity Trading Advisors On Form Pf	3235-AK92/ 3038-AD03	76 Fed. Reg. 71,128	SEC/CFTC
Securities And Exchange Commission: Net Worth Standard For Accredited Investors	3235-AK90	76 Fed. Reg. 81,793	SEC
Securities And Exchange Commission: Investment Adviser Performance Compensation	3235-AK71	77 Fed. Reg. 10,358	SEC
Securities And Exchange Commission: Consolidated Audit Trail	3235-AK51	77 Fed. Reg. 45,722	SEC
Securities And Exchange Commission: Disclosure Of Payments By Resource Extraction Issuers	3235–AK85	77 Fed. Reg. 56,365	SEC
Securities And Exchange Commission: Conflict Minerals	3235-AK84	77 Fed. Reg. 56,274	SEC

Source: GAO review of regulations from the *Federal Register.* | GAO-14-714

Appendix III: Selected Statistics from Rule Review

All estimates provided in this appendix for significant and economically significant rules are presented along with their margins of error, at the 95 percent confidence level. Values provided for major rules issued by independent regulatory agencies are population values: they are not estimates and are not subject to sampling error.

Table 7: Federal Rules That Included a Statement of Purpose by Rule Type - July 1, 2011 to June 30, 2013

Type of rule	Summary statistic	Included a statement of purpose	Did not include a statement of purpose
Economically significant	Percent of rules reviewed	100	0
	Unweighted frequency	57	0
	Margin of error (±)	5.12	5.12
Significant	Percent of rules reviewed	100	0
	Unweighted frequency	109	0
	Margin of error (±)	2.71	2.71
Major	Percent of rules reviewed	100	0
	Frequency	37	0

Source: GAO analysis of final regulations issued by executive and independent regulatory agencies. | GAO-14-714.

Table 8: Federal Rules with Monetized Costs by Rule Type - July 1, 2011 to June 30, 2013

Type of rule	Summary statistic	Costs monetized	Costs not monetized
Economically significant	Percent of rules reviewed	96.58	3.42
	Unweighted frequency	55	2
	Margin of error (±)	3.42	3.42
Significant	Percent of rules reviewed	38.53	61.47
	Unweighted frequency	42	67
	Margin of error (±)	7.04	7.04
Major	Percent of rules reviewed	78.38	21.62
	Frequency	29	8

Source: GAO analysis of final regulations issued by executive and independent regulatory agencies. | GAO-14-714.

Table 9: Federal Rules with Monetized Benefits by Rule Type - July 1, 2011 to June 30, 2013

Type of rule	Summary statistic	Benefits monetized	Benefits not monetized
Economically significant	Percent of rules reviewed	76.09	23.91
	Unweighted frequency	43	14
	Margin of error (±)	5.87	5.87
Significant	Percent of rules reviewed	15.60	84.40
	Unweighted frequency	17	92
	Margin of error (±)	6.07	6.07
Major	Percent of rules reviewed	5.41	94.59
	Frequency	2	35

Source: GAO analysis of final regulations issued by executive and independent regulatory agencies. | GAO-14-714.

Table 10: Pattern Analysis Showing Presence of Identified, Quantified, and Monetized Costs in Reviewed Economically Significant Rules - July 1, 2011 to June 30, 2013

Pattern (yes, no) analysis of identified, quantified, and monetized costs					
Costs					
Identified	Quantified	Monetized	Frequency	Percent of total	Margin of error (±)
No	No	Yes	24	42.31	7.20
Yes	No	Yes	22	37.58	6.81
Yes	Yes	Yes	5	8.54	4.63
No	Yes	Yes	4	8.15	6.81
No	Yes	No	1	1.71	2.79
Yes	No	No	1	1.71	2.79
Total			**57**	**100**	

Source: GAO analysis of final economically significant regulations issued by executive agencies. | GAO-14-714.

Table 11: Pattern Analysis Showing Presence of Identified, Quantified, and Monetized Benefits in Reviewed Economically Significant Rules - July 1, 2011 to June 30, 2013

Pattern (yes, no) analysis of identified, quantified, and monetized benefits

			Benefits		
Identified	Quantified	Monetized	Frequency	Percent of total	Margin of error (±)
Yes	No	Yes	18	32.07	6.92
No	No	Yes	11	20.11	7.13
Yes	No	No	11	18.79	6.02
Yes	Yes	Yes	8	13.66	5.43
No	Yes	Yes	6	10.25	4.93
Yes	Yes	No	3	5.12	3.89
Total			**57**	**100**	

Source: GAO analysis of final economically significant regulations issued by executive agencies. | GAO-14-714.

Table 12: Pattern Analysis Showing Presence of Identified, Quantified, and Monetized Costs in Reviewed Significant Rules - July 1, 2011 to June 30, 2013

Pattern (yes, no) analysis of identified, quantified, and monetized costs

			Costs		
Identified	Quantified	Monetized	Frequency	Percent of total	Margin of error (±)
No	No	No	47	43.12	7.16
No	No	Yes	25	22.94	6.08
Yes	No	No	14	12.84	5.72
Yes	No	Yes	7	6.42	4.57
Yes	Yes	Yes	7	6.42	4.57
Yes	Yes	No	4	3.67	3.84
No	Yes	Yes	3	2.75	3.53
No	Yes	No	2	1.83	3.16
Total			**109**	**100**	

Source: GAO analysis of final significant regulations issued by executive agencies. | GAO-14-714.

Note: Percentages may not total to 100 due to rounding.

Table 13: Pattern Analysis Showing Presence of Identified, Quantified, and Monetized Benefits in Reviewed Significant Rules - July 1, 2011 to June 30, 2013

Pattern (yes, no) analysis of identified, quantified, and monetized benefits

		Benefits			
Identified	Quantified	Monetized	Frequency	Percent of total	Margin of error (±)
Yes	No	No	45	41.28	7.12
No	No	No	37	33.94	6.85
Yes	Yes	No	10	9.17	5.13
Yes	No	Yes	9	8.26	4.96
No	No	Yes	4	3.67	3.84
No	Yes	Yes	2	1.83	3.16
Yes	Yes	Yes	2	1.83	3.16
Total			109	100	

Source: GAO analysis of final significant regulations issued by executive agencies. | GAO-14-714.

Note: Percentages may not total to 100 due to rounding.

Table 14: Pattern Analysis Showing Presence of Identified, Quantified, and Monetized Costs in Reviewed Major Rules - July 1, 2011 to June 30, 2013

Pattern (yes, no) analysis of identified, quantified, and monetized costs

		Costs		
Identified	Quantified	Monetized	Frequency	Percent of total
Yes	No	Yes	20	54.05
Yes	Yes	Yes	7	18.92
Yes	No	No	4	10.81
Yes	Yes	No	3	8.11
No	No	No	1	2.70
No	No	Yes	1	2.70
No	Yes	Yes	1	2.70
Total			37	100

Source: GAO analysis of final major regulations issued by independent regulatory agencies. | GAO-14-714.

Note: Percentages may not total to 100 due to rounding.

Table 15: Pattern Analysis Showing Presence of Identified, Quantified, and Monetized Benefits in Reviewed Major Rules - July 1, 2011 to June 30, 2013

Pattern (yes, no) analysis of identified, quantified, and monetized benefits				
Benefits				
Identified	Quantified	Monetized	Frequency	Percent of total
Yes	No	No	32	86.49
No	No	No	3	8.11
Yes	No	Yes	1	2.70
Yes	Yes	Yes	1	2.70
Total			**37**	**100**

Source: GAO analysis of final major regulations issued by independent regulatory agencies. | GAO-14-714.

Table 16: Federal Rules with Calculation of Net Benefits by Rule Type - July 1, 2011 to June 30, 2013

Type of rule	Summary statistic	With net benefits calculated	With no net benefits calculated
Economically significant	Percent of rules reviewed	37.19	62.81
	Unweighted frequency	21	36
	Margin of error (±)	7.09	7.09
Significant	Percent of rules reviewed	5.50	94.50
	Unweighted frequency	6	103
	Margin of error (±)	4.35	4.35
Major	Percent of rules reviewed	0	100
	Frequency	0	37

Source: GAO analysis of final regulations issued by executive and independent regulatory agencies. | GAO-14-714.

Table 17: Rules with Costs Identified, Quantified, or Monetized by Rule Type - July 1, 2011 to June 30, 2013

Type of rule	Summary statistic	With costs identified, quantified, or monetized	With no costs identified, quantified, or monetized
Economically significant	Percent of rules reviewed	100	0
	Unweighted frequency	57	0
	Margin of error (±)	5.12	5.12
Significant	Percent of rules reviewed	56.88	43.12
	Unweighted frequency	62	47
	Margin of error (±)	7.16	7.16
Major	Percent of rules reviewed	97.30	2.70
	Frequency	36	1

Source: GAO analysis of final regulations issued by executive and independent regulatory agencies. | GAO-14-714.

Table 18: Rules with Benefits Identified, Quantified, or Monetized by Rule Type - July 1, 2011 to June 30, 2013

Type of rule	Summary statistic	With benefits identified, quantified, or monetized	With no benefits identified, quantified, or monetized
Economically significant	Percent of rules reviewed	100	0
	Unweighted frequency	57	0
	Margin of error (±)	5.12	5.12
Significant	Percent of rules reviewed	66.06	33.94
	Unweighted frequency	72	37
	Margin of error (±)	6.85	6.85
Major	Percent of rules reviewed	91.89	8.11
	Frequency	34	3

Source: GAO analysis of final regulations issued by executive and independent regulatory agencies. | GAO-14-714.

Table 19: Rules That Identified Alternatives by Rule Type - July 1, 2011 to June 30, 2013

Type of rule	Summary statistic	Identified alternatives	Did not identify alternatives
Economically significant	Percent of rules reviewed	81.21	18.79
	Unweighted frequency	46	11
	Margin of error (±)	6.02	6.02
Significant	Percent of rules reviewed	22.02	77.98
	Unweighted frequency	24	85
	Margin of error (±)	5.99	5.99
Major	Percent of rules reviewed	62.16	37.84
	Frequency	23	14

Source: GAO analysis of final regulations issued by executive and independent regulatory agencies. | GAO-14-714.

Appendix IV: Rule Type Definitions for Executive Agency Rules

The following presents the definitions of the three rule types and the statute and executive order that define them (see figure 1), and includes the figure's rollover information.

Rule Types and the Statute and Executive Order That Define Them

Rule Types

Major Rule

A **major rule** is a rule that will likely result in an annual effect on the economy of $100 million or more, major increases in costs or prices, or a significant adverse effect on competition (including foreign competition), employment, productivity, or innovation. Both executive and independent regulatory agencies can issue major rules.

Significant Rule

A **significant rule** is a rule issued by an executive agency that fits one of the following three criteria:

- the rule is likely to create a serious inconsistency or otherwise interfere with an action taken or planned by another agency;
- the rule is likely to materially alter the budgetary impact of entitlements, grants, user fees, or loan programs or the rights and obligations of recipients thereof; or
- the rule is likely to raise novel legal or policy issues arising out of legal mandates, the President's priorities, or the principles set forth in Executive Order 12866.

Economically Significant Rule

An **economically significant rule** represents a subset of significant rules and includes rules that are likely to have an annual effect on the economy of $100 million or more or adversely affect in a material way the economy, a sector of the economy, productivity, competition, jobs, the environment, public health or safety, or state, local, or tribal government communities. Like significant rules, economically significant rules can be issued only by executive agencies.

Statute and Executive Order

The Congressional Review Act defines major rules and applies to rules issued by both executive and independent regulatory agencies.

Executive Order 12866 defines how rules issued by executive agencies are categorized as being either significant or economically significant. This executive order does not apply to independent regulatory agencies.

Appendix V: GAO Contact and Staff Acknowledgments

GAO Contact

Michelle Sager, (202) 512-6806 or sagerm@gao.gov

Staff Acknowledgments

In addition to the contact named above, Tara Carter, Assistant Director; Tom Beall, Tim Bober, Sara Daleski, Joseph Fread, Robert Gebhart, Tim Guinane, Shirley Hwang, Andrea Levine, Danielle Novak, Mark Ramage, Robert Robinson, and Alan Rozzi made key contributions to this report.

GAO's Mission	The Government Accountability Office, the audit, evaluation, and investigative arm of Congress, exists to support Congress in meeting its constitutional responsibilities and to help improve the performance and accountability of the federal government for the American people. GAO examines the use of public funds; evaluates federal programs and policies; and provides analyses, recommendations, and other assistance to help Congress make informed oversight, policy, and funding decisions. GAO's commitment to good government is reflected in its core values of accountability, integrity, and reliability.
Obtaining Copies of GAO Reports and Testimony	The fastest and easiest way to obtain copies of GAO documents at no cost is through GAO's website (http://www.gao.gov). Each weekday afternoon, GAO posts on its website newly released reports, testimony, and correspondence. To have GAO e-mail you a list of newly posted products, go to http://www.gao.gov and select "E-mail Updates."
Order by Phone	The price of each GAO publication reflects GAO's actual cost of production and distribution and depends on the number of pages in the publication and whether the publication is printed in color or black and white. Pricing and ordering information is posted on GAO's website, http://www.gao.gov/ordering.htm. Place orders by calling (202) 512-6000, toll free (866) 801-7077, or TDD (202) 512-2537. Orders may be paid for using American Express, Discover Card, MasterCard, Visa, check, or money order. Call for additional information.
Connect with GAO	Connect with GAO on Facebook, Flickr, Twitter, and YouTube. Subscribe to our RSS Feeds or E-mail Updates. Listen to our Podcasts. Visit GAO on the web at www.gao.gov.
To Report Fraud, Waste, and Abuse in Federal Programs	Contact: Website: http://www.gao.gov/fraudnet/fraudnet.htm E-mail: fraudnet@gao.gov Automated answering system: (800) 424-5454 or (202) 512-7470
Congressional Relations	Katherine Siggerud, Managing Director, siggerudk@gao.gov, (202) 512-4400, U.S. Government Accountability Office, 441 G Street NW, Room 7125, Washington, DC 20548
Public Affairs	Chuck Young, Managing Director, youngc1@gao.gov, (202) 512-4800 U.S. Government Accountability Office, 441 G Street NW, Room 7149 Washington, DC 20548

Please Print on Recycled Paper.

www.ingramcontent.com/pod-product-compliance
Lightning Source LLC
Chambersburg PA
CBHW080537290526
45790CB00006B/2439